LEARN SPANISH THE
GRINGA WAY

LEARN SPANISH THE GRINGA WAY

"THE EASIEST WAY FOR ENGLISH SPEAKERS TO LEARN SPANISH"

VOLUME 1

ERIN ASHLEY SIEBER

authorHOUSE®

AuthorHouse™
1663 Liberty Drive
Bloomington, IN 47403
www.authorhouse.com
Phone: 1-800-839-8640

Published by AuthorHouse   10/09/2014

ISBN: 978-1-4969-2436-0 (sc)
ISBN: 978-1-4969-2437-7 (e)

Copyediting - Karen Acevedo

Library of Congress Control Number: 2014913374

Author's Acknowledgments

In Loving Memory of Calvin Ginnavan

First and foremost this book would not have been possible without my very loving and supporting family. A special thank you to my mother Gail and my grandmother Ann, who are the wind beneath my wings and my biggest supporters. They have encouraged me to live my dreams and make my own path in life and supported me along each step of the way! For this there are no words that can express my amount of thanks.

Thank you to my very supportive husband who has always believed in me and supported my dream and passion for this book and has been patient with me every step of the way.

Word to fellow gringos

This book was written out of love for you, mi gente (my people)! As a fellow English speaker, I know how hard it is and how much effort it takes to learn Spanish, especially coming from a small town in the United States where no one speaks Spanish! After years of studying and living the language, I want to share my knowledge with you, saving you from years of hard work. This book is meant to be a useful tool for you, providing you with information in a unique and straightforward way! **It is possible** for gringos to learn Spanish!!!! You just need to learn it from…..

The Gringa!

The Gringo Oath

Yes we are Gringos
Yes we embrace the word
Yes we can and will learn Spanish!!!!!!!!

Su amiga, *The Gringa*!

TABLE OF CONTENTS

Phase 1

Phase 2

Phase 3

Phase 4

Phase 5

Icons used in this book

 This icon serves as a reminder

 This icon provides you with tips on learning

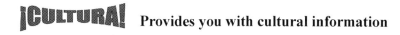 Provides you with cultural information

 This icon serves to give you caution/warning tips

ABOUT THE AUTHOR

Hi. Hola! My name is Erin and I am a gringa. Yes that is correct, a gringa. I decided to write this book to reach out to my fellow gringos (as) that are native English speakers but want to learn Spanish in an easy way. **_Whow you say… there is an easier way?_**

Let me begin by providing you with information on my background. I come from a very small American town called Ocean City, Maryland. My Grandfather, bless his soul, always used to say that it was "the best place in the world". I agree with him. It is a wonderful town but it is small and not that culturally robust. I grew up not ever hearing a word of any other language, other than English. Until I started traveling, I am not as sure to what extent I realized the complexity of the world out there; where people spoke different languages and lived different ways of life. In general, my personal experience has been that a lot of people here in the states think that anyone who speaks Spanish comes from Mexico, not understanding or stopping to think that they could be from one of the other 20 countries where Spanish is the national language. I don't say this in a negative way at all; it is just the way it is. And again, I say this from actual "real life" experience.

It wasn't until I was fourteen years old and I was given a trip to Cancun, Mexico for Christmas, that I probably thought the same way too. Yes it was this trip that changed the rest of my career course and really my outlook on life and other cultures.

What happened you ask? Well, I arrived to Cancun young and ready to explore the new land. In other words, young, first time out of the United States and ready to mingle! Being at an age where you do start liking boys, my girlfriend and I met four boys from Argentina and took a liking to them, from the visual standpoint at first. Out of the four boys only one could somewhat speak enough English to communicate in a basic sense. The others, one of which was the one I took a fancy to, did not speak a word of English. One night we were sitting in the lobby with them trying to get to know them. The one problem with this scenario? None of us spoke each other's language. I was just about to enter my freshman year in high school, which is when you had to choose what language you would take until you graduated, and therefore had not studied any Spanish (besides knowing how to say "hola" and "tequila"). My best friend (shout out to Kristie), who was with me on the trip, had one year of Spanish under her belt but was not advanced in any sense of the term. She could say what our names were and how old we were but that was about it. What is the point of this story you ask? Well, it was in the moment of pure frustration and disappointment of *not being able to communicate* with another human being (and one that I was interested in at that), that I told myself I would not let that happen again. It was at that moment that I said that not only was I going to go back to the Unites States, choose Spanish as my language of choice for my high school career but I was going to go on to major in the Spanish language in college and then obtain a career using Spanish.

Most people back home doubted me and thought I was crazy when I would say this, chalking it up to being young and not knowing what you want or thinking that there was too much time in between my freshman year of high school and my freshman year of college to even remotely be able to decide what major I was going to take. Others said that people usually don't even know what they want to major in when they start college and others wondered what I was going to do with a Bachelor's degree in Spanish. What happened? I did just what I said I was going to do that night in the lobby in our hotel in Cancun, Mexico. I went on to take four years of Spanish in high school and was inducted in the Spanish National Honor Society. I then went on to major in Spanish right from the start of my freshman year at Florida Atlantic University. I studied two semesters abroad. I went through my University for a three-month program in Salamanca, Spain and then returned again for another three months at the private Estudio Sampere Language School en El Puerto de Santa Maria and Salamanca, Spain and then returned to the US to graduate with a Bachelor in Spanish and a certification in International Business.

Let me take a pause out of where I am present day and talk about the study abroad program I did and how instrumental it was in my learning Spanish. Prior to hopping on the 747 to cross the Atlantic Ocean and arrive in foreign soil to learn Spanish and live amongst a different culture, I had only learned Spanish in the classroom. I had been to Spain one time before in high school but was now returning as a college adult ready to intensify my Spanish. The day I landed in Spain back in 1999, I began with what became a surreal chapter in my life and in my Spanish career. Interestingly enough, I was one of the "tryouts" for a new exchange program between my college and a business college in Spain. The location where I would be living and taking classes was at an all-boys seminary. I thought it was very interesting that they would allow girls from the US to room and board at an all-boys seminary but didn't question it. It only got better as far as I was concerned when I found out that it also served as the dorm quarters for boy students from the University of Salamanca. It literally turned out to be a coed international exchange program. This helped tremendously on the cultural aspect of the program. Living with people of a different culture is a very beneficial aspect of life experiences, as well as learning cultural differences and opinions, some very stereotypical, others not. It is amazing how different people view others from different cultures. I remember sitting in "la sala" or the "living room" the first week I arrived watching the Spanish students watch an American program on television. They had a lot of stereotypes already set in their mind of what

American life was like. I have to admit, a lot of stereotypes are true, as they are in any culture. The beauty about what they would talk about was from a perspective of never having actually traveled to the United States, but instead it was what they had watched on television. These points of views and others will become relevant as I move forward in the book, illustrating why it is important to know that there is a vast world out there with different ways of life and different views of things.

Okay, well, now let me tell you how I succeeded in following the dream I had 15 years ago as I returned from Mexico and entered high school. When I graduated from Florida Atlantic University in Boca Raton, Florida, I knew that I could not return home to Ocean City, Maryland and expect to retain the Spanish I had worked very hard to learn. In fact, the summer I graduated from college, I went home and I needed to hear some Spanish so I wouldn't forget the language. I called the cable company to try and order a Spanish television program. I was flabbergasted when they told me that they would not have the capability to transmit a Spanish show in town until the year 2010. I knew that I was living in Gringoville USA and in order to continue with my Spanish, I needed to move back to Spain or move to Miami, Florida (which was only about an hour from where I went to college). I decided to move to Miami since it was a much closer move at the time. I didn't really know anyone there but I just packed up the moving truck, made a couple of trips, and unloaded at my new apartment. I have not been disappointed ever since with my decision. Miami, FL really is a world unto itself in the United States. It is a place you have to experience in order to believe life really exists that way. It does not matter where I go, I always here someone speaking Spanish. For me, this is exactly what I wanted. I thought to myself, what is the second best thing to actually living in a Spanish speaking country….Miami, Florida! It is very true too. The culture, the people, the way of life, the language all revolve around the Latin culture and Spanish is spoken everywhere. I feel like I was ten years before my time because learning Spanish has really been a key, if not the determining factor in why I have obtained the jobs I have in Miami. Basically, almost every job requires that you be bilingual. There are a lot of second and third generations Latino's living in Miami who grew up hearing and speaking Spanish in the home and then learned English in school and therefore speak English as well. I have had to compete against these people just to qualify for the same job even though I didn't have the advantage of hearing Spanish growing up. I had to learn Spanish from the word "hola" or "hi" and have learned it fluently since then.

I can't forget the day I was called by the Miami Herald, a very large newspaper company in Florida, in regards to a resume I had submitted. I didn't even really remember the job that I had applied for when I was called back but I was pleasantly surprised to hear that it was for El Nuevo Herald, the Spanish sister paper of the Miami Herald. The job position was for the Business Development Manager, basically managing and promoting the Hispanic market through education of the importance of the Hispanic Market. I thought it was my dream job, as I had always wanted a job that dealt with the Hispanic culture (since that is, after all, what I went to school to study) and a job where speaking Spanish was a requirement. The day I went in for my first interview, I had practiced my Spanish, knowing that Spanish was a requirement for the job and also knowing that once the interviewer took one look at me they were going to think "this girl can't know how to speak Spanish, she can probably only say hello and goodbye". I say this because in fact the very vast majority of Americans do not speak Spanish. I hesitate to say it but it is almost understood amongst the Hispanic culture that an American probably does not know any, or if best, only a little Spanish. This is exactly what happened in my interview. During the first part of it we spoke in English and as I was waiting for the moment to be tested, then it came. The man in charge, my future boss, politely asked if I would mind speaking in Spanish for the rest of the interview. Of course I said, not a problem and continued on with the interview in Spanish. Needless to say, I got the job; a job that I can honestly say was my dream job at the time. I was very happy and proud that I was offered the job. I was the only non-Hispanic person working for El Nuevo Herald. Everyone was intrigued when I first started that I was an American that had been hired to work for a Spanish newspaper and that I actually spoke Spanish fluently. I have to admit that in the beginning people were a little curious as to how I landed the job. It makes you learn quickly in life that people never you give you the credit you deserve until you prove yourself and show them what you are made of. That is exactly what I had to do in that position. It turned out to be a great job and I wouldn't have gotten it had I not been **bilingual.**

Okay, well hopefully by now I have shared enough of my background and my journey to give you an insight as to how a "gringa" can go from not knowing how to even say "hi" in Spanish to working for one of the largest Spanish papers in the country and speaking Spanish fluently. I wanted to give you this insight to let you know *that if you want something bad enough, all you have to do is put your mind to it, go out and do it and ignore skepticism of others along the way*.

THE GRINGA WAY

The Gringa Way is a **5 Phase Principle and 5 Phase Method** designed specifically for *native English speaking* people who want to learn usable Spanish without the headaches, and years of frustration spent in a traditional classroom setting with stacks and stacks of grammar books. **The Gringa Way** provides students the ability to learn the Spanish language from the ground up, learning the basics and working your way forward, phase by phase. The technique emphasizes correlating the **Spanish language** to our native **English language**, making it easier for you to see and learn exactly how you need to look at the language from our native tongue, and then relate it to the **Spanish** language.

The Gringa Way 5 Principles:

1. **Relate your native English language to learning Spanish** - this is the foundation of the The Gringa Way. Most Spanish teaching is geared towards getting you to think in Spanish and forgetting your English language while learning Spanish. However, if you don't think about how to relate what you are learning and how to compare the language that you already know (English) to the one you are trying to learn (Spanish), how will you be able to make sense out of it? That is why The Gringa Way focuses all learning of the Spanish language to things that you can relate to in English, therefore helping you make more sense out of it!

2. **Reading, Listening, Speaking, Writing** - This is the order that The Gringa Way emphasizes learning the Spanish language. Most schools around the world teach reading first, then writing, then listening and finally speaking. This is probably why, even if you have learned vocabulary or Spanish grammar before, you are afraid to speak because you are afraid of not saying something correct. Speaking is the most crucial part of a language, and for second language acquisition, the hardest. It is the most crucial because you have to speak to people in order to communicate. Of course you could always write down each thing you want to say on a piece of

paper and hand it to people but you and I both know that doesn't happen and in reality, can't work effectively. Therefore, you have to know how to speak! It is the hardest part of learning a second language because it takes more brain effort, due to the fact that you need to remember what you have read and learned and you need to do so faster (unlike writing where you have enough time to write down your thoughts, check your text for errors, erase if incorrect, etc.). To give you an example, I took 4 to 5 years of Spanish before I entered a classroom where we were actually asked to speak and give oral answers and opinions, instead of just listening to the teacher talk.

3. **Practice Out Loud, *Don't Just Read!*** This is very important and you should adapt this principle from the time you read the first Spanish word in this book. As mentioned in principle two, if you just read and do not speak, you will feel inhibited when you finally try to speak. You should practice saying every word out loud, this way you will train both your brain and your mouth, allowing both of them to help you communicate verbally!

4. **Do not Translate Word for Word** - Spanish is a very literal language (which will be covered in this book) but it cannot always be translated literally from English. You need to encompass the Spanish language as an overall whole. Once you see the big picture, you will realize the importance of not always translating word for word!

5. **Motivation & Memory** - These are the key ingredients you must have and continue to use throughout your Spanish language learning journey. Motivation is numero uno! You must be motivated to learn. Even if you are being forced to learn for a certain reason; i.e. a mandatory class in high school or college, in order to obtain a new job, receive a promotion, etc. you must continue your motivation! Memorizing and remembering what you are learning is key to retention, which ultimately provides you with your knowledge. Last but not least, you need to PRACTICE! Think about sports players or Olympians....do you think they get to be as good as they are without practice? Not a chance! They dedicate so much of their time to practicing their speciality. That is why they get so good at it!

Repetition is a very useful tool when learning a language. After all, practice makes perfect. If you continually see something over and over and you continuously study something over and over, eventually, you will come to memorize it. Take for example your vocabulary class back in grade school. I remember having to memorize English vocabulary in order to pass tests and quizzes. Ultimately, I remembered the words. Also, think of your favorite songs that you listen to and sing along with. At some point, either through constant repetition of playing these songs or listening closely each time they play, you eventually remember the words.

THE GRINGA WAY FIVE PHASES:

Phase 1 - Introduction to Basics

The Introduction phase serves to introduce you to the language, as well as to its most basic elements of the Spanish language. The idea is to start with very simple and basic concepts and relate them to the English language. This will provide you with an easier way to correlate the learning of Spanish to English.

In this phase, you will be exposed to:

- The alphabet
- Numbers
- Days of the week
- Months
- Seasons
- Telling Time
- Colors

You will be introduced to some patterns. A pattern is a type of theme of recurring events or objects. The goal is to start seeing and understanding patterns in the language because this will help you compute the language better and can make it easier for you to move on to more advance concepts.

Phase 2 - Basics

The Basics phase continues to build on from the Introduction phase and introduces you to more basic elements of the language. This phase is important because you have already been exposed to the most elemental components of a language and now begin learning more concepts.

In this phase you will be exposed to:

- Literal aspects of Spanish
- Word stress
- Spanish you already know
- Mirror Images
- Suffixes

Phase 3 - Basics Intermediate

This phase is where you will start to advance a little more with your Spanish. It is where you should begin to be able to start using your retention of the basics to help you see the language more clearly.

In this phase, you will be exposed to:

- Masculine and feminine concept
- Determiners
- The Who
- Possession

The Gringa Way suggests making stickers, signs or sticky notes (whetever works best for you) and labeling many commonly used items in your house; from the mirror you look into when getting ready, to your water glass, coffee mug, television, etc. with the corresponding Spanish word. Although this might seem trivial, you will notice that you become more and more familiar with these words subconsciously. They will become "less foreign to you" and you will absorb these words and arrive at a point when you know them without even thinking about them! This is what The Gringa Way refers to as "Subliminal Absorption".

Phase 4 - Intermediate

The Intermediate phase is where you really start getting further into the core of the language and start learning items that will advance your availability to be able to speak. This phase contains a lot of the "meat and potatoes" of the language and also contains some of the most confusing items for English speakers. This section will baffle you at first and even frustrate you but it is imperative that you learn the items in this phase backwards and forward.

In this phase you will be exposed to:

- Questions
- Describing
- Por vs. Para
- Ser vs. Estar

The goal of this phase is to be able to:

• Improve comprehension
• Be able to describe and explain
• Summarize

Phase 5 - Advanced

This is the last phase and it really is the pinnacle of your Spanish language acquisition. Not only will you be exposed to one of the most important areas of the Spanish language but also one of the most difficult to learn, verbs. This is a very crucial phase, as you will not only learn items that are needed in order to speak in a Spanish sentence but you will also learn how to form a sentence. You will be able to incorporate everything you have learned in phase 1- 4 in this phase as well.

In this phase you will be exposed to:

- Action words
- Se
- Commands
- Spanish sentences
- Other ways to speak
- Commonly confused words

The goal of this phase is to be able to:

- Give opinions
- Have adequate face-to-face conversations
- Conversational proficiency

The Gringa Way requires that you **REPEAT EACH CHAPTER 5 TIMES** before moving on to the next Chapter. Why? Because the more you review the material, the more you will not only come to absorb it but the more it will make sense to you! I don't want you just cruising through the chapters without retaining the information; retention is the key to learning!

INTRODUCTION

Spanish in the World

DID YOU KNOW?

- Spanish is a national language in 20 sovereign states and one dependent entity. (http://en.wikipedia.org/wiki/List_of_countries_where_Spanish_is_an_official_language)

- There are 53 million Hispanics in the United States as of July 1, 2012, making people of Hispanic origin the nation's largest ethnic or racial minority. Hispanics constituted 17 percent of the nation's total population. (Source: **US Census Bureau 2012)**
- "Bilingual employees earn, on average, between 5-20 percent more per hour than the position's base rate." (Source: **Salary.com)**

- 50 percent of recruiters say that, all else being equal, they prefer hiring employees who are proficient in Spanish or Mandarin." (Source: http://www.careerbuilder.com/Article/CB-163-Getting-Ahead-Bilingual-Youre-Valuable)

FOOD for Thought

Why Bother Learning Spanish?

The most spoken language in the world is Mandarin Chinese followed by English then Spanish. Since you are already English speakers, then being able to speak Spanish would make you able to speak with more than half the population of the world, as well as open doors to a lot more opportunities for you! Luckily, for us native English speakers, Spanish is much more closely related to English then Mandarin Chinese! Here is a perfect ejemplo:

I want chocolate:

Chinese: 我要巧克力 **Spanish:** Quiero chocolate

I rest my case, Learn Spanish!

The History of the Word Gringo

What is a gringo (a)?

I am sure you have heard this term before, in fact, you might have even been called this before. Some Americans might take some offense to this term, some not. I personally do not find it offensive at all. Which is why I included this section about the origin of the term. I think it is important to understand how someone or a group of people, arrive at a point where they can generally use a term or nickname for a group of people. If you are ever going to be called a gringo (a), you might as well know the history behind it.

Gringo (feminine, **gringa,** *hence the name of the book*) is a Spanish and Portuguese word used in Latin America to generally denote people from the United States, but in some cases it is also used to denote foreign non-native speakers of Spanish (physical appearance i.e. race often plays a role), usually from northern Europe or Canada-especially English-speakers.

Folk etymologies (change in a word or phrase over time resulting from the replacement of an unfamiliar form by a more familiar one). There are many popular but unsupported etymologies for this word, some of which relate it to the United States Army.

Mexican-American War

In the years preceding the Mexican-American War, Irish-Americans in the United States were extremely persecuted. The intolerance was so great that when the Mexican-American War began, many Irish-Americans fought on the side of Mexico, because the Mexicans were much more tolerant of the Irish because both groups were Catholics. Green is the color of the Irish and one of the favorite marching songs of the Irish soldiers was a tune called "Green Grow the Lilacs, Oh!" Eventually, the term "Gringo" (Green Go) arose from these encounters and was used to refer to people from the United States. This etymology is usually hidden because the persecution of the Irish in America is a subject unfriendly to those who don't want the world to know that white people were also persecuted in the United States.

A more popular theory among Mexicans is derived from the lack of popularity of the American dollar (also called green) in those days due to many undetermined reasons (for ejemplo, a weak dollar compared to the Mexican peso). When Americans wanted to use their dollars in Mexico, people did not accept those, saying "green, go", which later was transformed into "gringo".

"Greek" hypothesis

According to the Catalan etymologist Joan Coromines, *gringo* is derived from *griego* (Spanish for "Greek"), the archetypal term for an unintelligible language (a usage found also in the Shakespearean "it was Greek to me" and its derivative "It's all Greek to me"). From referring simply to language, it was extended to people speaking foreign tongues and to their physical features.

Gringolandia

The word *Gringolandia* (Gringoland) is a mock, single-word name for the *United States of America*. *Gringolandia* derives from the compounding of the words "gringo" and "-landia" (land of) into this term. This composition was inspired by the word Disneyland (from the name Disney and the word land), which in Spanish was translated as Disneylandia. Walt Disney's movies and cartoons have always been popular in Mexico, and they inspired the mock name "Gringolandia."

The term is also used by natives of Quito, Ecuador to describe a sector of the city called La Mariscal. This neighborhood is the entertainment and tourism hub of Quito, and subsequently attracts many foreigners. Hotels, restaurants, bars, and shops in La Mariscal cater to tourists, students, expats, and business travelers coming from many parts of the world, particularly from English-speaking countries, and so it is jokingly nicknamed *Gringolandia*. (Source: http://en.wikipedia.org/wiki/Gringo)

What side are you on?

I am sure most of you reading this book have heard of the right brain/left brain theory. According to the theory of left-brain or right-brain dominance, each side of the brain controls different types of thinking. People are said to prefer one type of thinking over the other. For example, a person who is "left-brained" is often said to be more logical, analytical and objective, while a person who is "right brained" is said to be more intuitive, thoughtful and subjective. I have always said that I am a "right brain" person because I do not like analysis that much and consider myself to be much more a creative person than an analytical one.

That being said, I feel that learning a language requires both sides of the brain, especially for native English speakers learning Spanish. It will require you to analyze similarities between English and Spanish and it will require you to analyze differences and to be creative and intuitive in doing all of these. So if you have ever considered yourself to be one side or the other, put that thought aside and tell yourself you are now about to *"Crisscross"* the two!

Now let the fun begin!

Inventions and new products are born from necessity! Necessity is how I arrived at writing this book. I have listened to fellow gringos that I either know or have met along the way tell me that they have taken years of Spanish and don't remember a thing! I kept thinking to myself, if native English speaker after native English speaker keeps telling me the same thing, there must be a reason why they are not learning or remembering the language. It is not like native English speakers are in capable of learning Spanish....this is not the reason! I will get to the reasons why in the following chapter, but right now I want to make a statement about this book. My intention is to teach you in a way that does not follow the norm textbook learning. I am not going to bore you with one big grammar word after another and I am also not going to put a timeframe on your learning of the language.

Now, whether or not this takes you 10 days or one year is up to YOU. Have you ever wondered how children pick up languages so easily? This is because children do not have a time frame when they are growing up and learning a new language. They do not have any pressure to learn the language their relatives are speaking by a certain age. They simply learn over time by hearing the people around them speaking. You may be use to or tired of seeing the phrase "Learn Spanish in 10 days" or "Be fluent in two months" etc. I do believe in intensive learning *but this book is for gringos who just want to learn usable Spanish.*

The advice I give to you is:

- **You must take learning the language SERIOUSLY**
- **You must be consistent in your studying**
- **You must really put your mind in it when you are studying**
- **You must tell yourself that you can learn it every time you pick up this book**
- **Please do not allow yourself to get interrupted** (as hard as it may be in this busy modern world) **while you read this book. Even if it is for 10 or 15 minutes a day, you must give full attention to learning!** *You must be focused and you must be consistent!!!!*

This book is really a "grass roots" approach to the language. My goal is for you to learn, or to at least have an understanding of the language in the simplest form and easiest way possible. This book is really to help my fellow gringos avoid the years of trying to make sense of Spanish and understand the language. You have to understand that Spanish is very different than English. It has many more verb tenses and tangible and intangible items have gender connotations, such as "**la** silla" for the chair and "**el** restaurante" for the restaurant. Who would have ever of thought that a chair was feminine and a restaurant was masculine? In English it is just **the** chair or **the** restaurant. Pretty simple, right? For years now I have heard people tell me that they studied Spanish for years in high school and didn't learn it or can only remember some words. There are other people who have told me that they know some words but don't know how to put any of them together to make a sentence and be able to talk. **My goal is to help you avoid the years of mental anguish trying to correlate English to Spanish and trying to make sense of it.** I have conquered that feat and now I want to make it as easy as I can for you to learn.

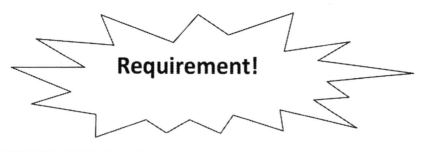

Requirement!

REPEAT EACH CHAPTER 5 TIMES BEFORE ADVANCING ON TO NEXT CHAPTER
REPEAT EACH CHAPTER 5 TIMES BEFORE ADVANCING ON TO NEXT CHAPTER
REPEAT EACH CHAPTER 5 TIMES BEFORE ADVANCING ON TO NEXT CHAPTER
REPEAT EACH CHAPTER 5 TIMES BEFORE ADVANCING ON TO NEXT CHAPTER
REPEAT EACH CHAPTER 5 TIMES BEFORE ADVANCING ON TO NEXT CHAPTER

The Gringa Way Phase 1

Capítulo uno (Chapter 1)

Change your Thinking, Change Your World.

This chapter is dedicated to really diving into your inner self (I know, sounds cheesy) but trust me when I tell you this is the most important start to learning a language. As I mentioned above, for years now I have heard people tell me that they have taken some Spanish courses but don't remember a word. My theory behind this is three fold.

Reason one: You probably didn't really want to. For most of you, you probably don't have a yearning burning desire to learn Spanish. You probably saw Spanish class as a mandatory class that you had to take a few years of in high school and just thought you would do the minimum you could to get by to pass the class. *Sound familiar?* My thought behind this, and really anything in life, is that if you don't really want to do something, you are not going to do it. For example, I do not like math at all. I always fought it during high school and even in college I did whatever I could to only take the bare minimum requirement. That worked out well until I went for my Masters in Business Administration and realized that most of the courses were math oriented. However, I wanted to get an MBA so bad that I told myself to snap out of it and put my mind to do the math requirements I had to in order to complete the program. It is really **mind over matter** because I was able to get through the math classes and get good grades. As the great Theodore Roosevelt once said, **"With self-discipline most anything is possible"**

Reason 2: I call this Philosophy **"Forgetta Bout it"**! As it is explained in the movie "Donnie Brasco". This is really the first step in your Spanish learning adventure. What do I mean by this? Well, as gringos, our minds are positioned in at certain way. A vast majority of us, unless you grew up in a major city where there was some sort of Latin presence, only heard English growing up. Aside from that, you might have had or still have preconceptions that English is the only language that you need to know in life and any other language isn't that important to learn. I am here to tell you that in order to dive into another language; you have to open your minds up to the fact that Spanish is a very important and useful language to learn, both presently and for the future!

Reason 3: Most of the time, probably the majority of the time, teachers, professors, online books, etc. are taught by native Spanish speakers. Native Spanish speakers never had to learn Spanish; just as us gringos (as) never had to learn English. Of course, we had to perfect our vocabulary and grammar throughout the course of schooling but that is merely an enhancement to a language, not the learning of a language from the beginning. As much respect as I have for all teachers and anyone teaching a foreign language, my feeling is this: If you never had to learn the foreign language you are trying to teach from the beginning, how can one know the anguish and frustration of the learning process from the word "hi" (*hola*) to the formation of a complete sentence? I had to struggle through the learning of each word and each grammar lesson and try to somehow relate the 'foreignness" of it to English. That is why I am writing this book. I want to share the ways I tried to learn Spanish through each process, in order to make it easier for you!

You have to tell yourself:

- ✓ That yes, it will be difficult
- ✓ You will get frustrated at some point along the way
- ✓ It may seem impossible at times throughout your learning curve
- ✓ That even though you might think you will never get to the point of being able to understand and speak it, that you can and will still put 150% effort towards continuing to try.

I have learned that learning a language is not just about learning grammar words and how to put sentences together on paper but rather it is your spoken communication skills that are of utmost importance. After all, the way you communicate with another person is verbally. People can be verbally fluent in their native language but not be able to read or write at all. However, in a second language acquisition, the majority of the time, a person can read and write the foreign language before they are able to communicate verbally. This is because the natural order of learning a language in your native tongue is listening, speaking, reading, and writing (which is how babies and children are able to learn a language without ever having to study). In regards to learning a foreign language, the general order taught is reading, listening, writing then speaking. **However, the key to learning a second language,** *verbal communication*, **is the hardest level.** As mentioned in the The Gringa Way 5 principles, when speaking with someone verbally, there is not time to use a translator or go back and correct a word because you have to speak on the spot! This is the reason that I feel a lot of people get frustrated and a lot of times even embarrassed. They are afraid that they are going to sound funny speaking it or that people are going to make fun of their pronunciation. Let me give you this word of advice....DO NOT BECOME ONE OF THESE STATISTCS. If you let yourself be afraid to speak and practice, you are not going to get to a level where you can communicate! Do you know how many Spanish speaking people speak English with an accent? A LOT. The bottom line is that they speak English and that they have learned the language. Unless you are a native Spanish speaker, chances are, you are not going to speak like one! As I mentioned, I studied in Spain and I learned "Castellano" with the Spanish Castilian accent. When I want to really put on a show, I break out my Castellano accent but most of the times, when I speak Spanish, it sounds like a gringa speaking (using proper pronunciation and accents of the words of course). But I can communicate and because I am pronouncing the words properly (very important), the lack of a native accent is not that important.

The purpose of this book is to enable you to communicate verbally. In order to be able to speak Spanish (and eventually fluently), you need to practice speaking! When you study, don't just read the material and say it to yourself in your mind. Say what you are reading, especially the pronunciation, OUT LOUD!

Learning a foreign language opens your world up to a whole new culture with unique ways of thinking and living, as well as to a new group of people that might think differently than what you are used to and can provide another outlook on life. I have learned this first hand and can tell you how rewarding it has been for me. I think about all of my friends that I have made in Miami that are Hispanic and how meeting them

5

and being in their life has opened up my world as to how people think differently, the different foods they like, the way their social gatherings are different, and so forth. It really is great being able to crossover and experience this other world and it is made possible because they know that, not only have I put in the effort to learn their language, but I have also taken the time to understand who they are as individuals and as a culture.

The most profound analogy I ever learned is *"when a boat is sinking, people start bailing out the water; however, what they fail to do is look for the hole, the source of the problem, to patch it up and stop the leaking"*. This correlates with language learning as well. A lot of times, people have the tendency to just hear words instead of paying close attention to what they are hearing. The purpose of this book is not to learn a lot of big grammar lessons that don't give any correlation back to your native English language, but rather to provide you with a way to be able to correlate English to Spanish and make the learning process and acquisition of the language clearer and easier. If you want to pass tests of grammar definitions, then study grammar. However, if you want to be able to speak to someone, then you should try to learn without studying too much grammar. Studying a lot of grammar will only slow you down and confuse you. You will think about the rules when creating sentences instead of naturally saying a sentence like a native. For example, the majority, if not a big percentage of native English speakers probably don't know what a preposition is, what a past participle verb is, what a gerund of a word is, yet they are fluent in English! Only a small fraction of English speakers know more than 20% of all the grammar rules. So I ask you, do you want to be able to recite the definition of a past participle verb, or do you want to be able to speak Spanish? If you understand the *root*, the foundation of a language, you will have a better outlook for learning the language as a whole.

The bottom line is; if you are reading this book, chances are you are not a native Spanish speaker and will not learn like one. In order to confirm this, ask yourself two questions:

- **Are you native?**
- **Do you think in Spanish?**

If you answered no, then you can rest assured that this book is geared towards you and for you in order to help you make the correlation between the English and Spanish languages. *The bottom line is that learning Spanish is not easier or harder than English, it's that it is completely different*!

¡CULTURA!

Café Cubano (Cuban coffee, Cuban espresso, cafecito, Cuban shot) is a type of espresso which originated in Cuba after espresso machines were first imported there from Italy. Specifically, it refers to an espresso shot which is sweetened with demerara sugar as it is being brewed, but the name covers other drinks that use Cuban espresso as their base. Drinking café cubano remains a prominent social and cultural activity within Cuba as well as the Cuban exile community (http://en.wikipedia.org/wiki/Cuban_espresso)

Cortadito - A Cuban drink that is a shot of espresso with a squirt of steamed milk and sugar or a very strong coffee that is 2/3 milk.

In Miami there are literally thousands of "cafeterías" where you can walk up to la ventana (the window) and order a café cubano. One of these little shots really hit the spot! Average cost is around $.75 to $1.25

Phonetics (from the Greek: φωνή, *phōnē*, "sound, voice") is a branch of linguistics that comprises the study of the sounds of human speech, It is concerned with the physical properties of speech sounds or signs (phones): their physiological production, acoustic properties, auditory perception, and neurophysiologic status! (Source: http://en.wikipedia.org/wiki/Phonetics)

What does the first part of this definition say? Greek...... Yes, the expression, **"It's all Greek to me"** holds true if you try to go by the phonetic pronunciation as a gringo (a) trying to learn Spanish. Basically, in my opinion, it is a language all to itself. Having a Spanish major in college, I had to take a phonetics class for a full semester. Wow, talk about feeling like I was in a washing machine by the time class let out! I literally didn't even know my name by the time class let out because phonetics and all the abstract concepts that encompass it, was such a foreign concept. How can you be expected to take on two languages at once? I am going to teach you a very simple English speaking approach to pronunciation and learning of the Spanish language. The Gringa Way DOES NOT use phonetics to demonstrate the pronunciation of a word. It uses just the opposite. It uses the English language to convey the pronunciation of each Spanish syllable and words.

How many words do you need to know in order to speak Spanish?

If you think about your average day, you might realize that your interaction with people consists of basic words that are used very often and repeated often. When you are talking about how your morning was, how traffic was driving to work, how your class at school was, what you did over the weekend etc., you communicate on a social basis with virtually the same basic vocabulary. On the flip side, however, if you are out with some friends for dinner and enter into a discussion about politics, the environment or any other specific topics of discussion, then you would most likely need to use some additional or advance vocabulary to express your thoughts and feelings about the topic. However, for the most part in daily life, your vocabulary is fairly basic. We, as people, tend to stick to the words we know. Some people claim that on an average day to day conversation in your own language, no more than 1,000 words are used, and that for more advanced speaking, using 3,000 words would be the most a person would use in any given day or week. Other people say that 50% of all spoken language consists of the 100 most common words in that language.

What is the point to this? The point is that in order to learn basic communication, you only need a certain amount of fundamental words and generalized conversational vocabulary in order to be able to talk to people on the street, in the grocery store, with your friends, etc. This is good news for you! Now, if you are planning on obtaining a bilingual job that requires Spanish or you are going to be focusing on communicating in a specialized field of some sort, then you will have to learn the basic vocabulary that pertains to that field as well, so that you can enhance your communication.

CAPÍTULO DOS (CHAPTER 2)

The Alphabet (el alfabeto) made simple!

English Alphabet	**Spanish Alphabet**

a b c d e f g h
i j k l m n o p q
r s t u v w x y z

a b c d e f g h i
j k l m n ñ o p q
r s t u v w x y z

Do you see any similarities between the English alphabet and the Spanish alphabet? I hope you can because the *good news is,* both the English and the Spanish alphabets use the "Latin alphabet", which is pictured above.

The English alphabet contains 26 letters. The Spanish alphabet contains 27 single letters (A-Z,) **with one additional letter, ñ** (Pronounced "N" + "YAAY"). There are also three letters in the Spanish alphabet, **ch, ll, rr,** which are traditionally not considered individual letters. **All letters are pronounced with the exception of the "h."**

Besides these three differences:

- the **ñ**
- the letters **ch, ll, rr**
- the silence of the **h**

The **pronunciation** is the only *main difference* between the alphabets.

The alphabet is for spelling and learning the sounds of the letters. As is in English, when letters are put together to form a word, they take on the pronunciation of the word in its entirety.

The letters are all feminine (I know, you are probably asking yourself how a letter can be feminine. I will explain this later; just go with it for now).

The Gringa Way to learning the alphabet is not to memorize each letter but to associate each letter and its pronunciation with that of an English word. Relating the pronunciation to an English sound and word will make it easier for you to correlate it.

Let's begin! ¡Vamos a empezar!

a- As in say **"ahhhhh"** (like when you are in the dentist chair)
b- Pronounced like the English word **"bay"** (As in the body of water)
c- Pronounced like the English word **"say"**
ch- Pronounced like the "ch" in the English words: **ch**ange, **ch**ile, **ch**ocolate
d- Pronounced like the English word **day**
e- Pronounced like the English letter "A"
f- Pronounced like the lette*r* "F" and "A" put together (F, A)
g- Pronounced like the English word **"hay"** (As in *hay* is for horse)

When the g precedes a, o, u, or a consonant, it is pronounced like a hard English g. (**agosto**) (AH-GO-STOW)

When the g precedes an e or i, it is pronounced like a Spanish J (**gente**) (HEN-TAY)

---

h- Pronounced "AH" "Chay"

The **h** in Spanish is **SILENT!** That is why the letter h is pronounced "AH-CHAY" instead of "HA-CHAY". Gringos (as) commonly mispronounce words that start with the letter h, such as pronouncing hacer (pronounced AH-SEAR), as (HA-SEAR) and hambre (pronounced AHM-BRAY) as (HAM-BRAY).

Remember: to say hi in Spanish is Hola pronounced 0-LAH, *NOT HOLE-AH*

i- Pronounced like the English letter **"E"**
j- This letter is a little funky. It is pronounced with the beginning sound of **"ho"** and followed by **"ta"** (hoe-ta)

The letter **"j"** is used for the sound provided by the letter *h in English*. Gringos (as) usually try and pronounce the j in Spanish as the English j. The most common word is probably jalapeño, commonly mispronounced as gel-a-pea-no. The correct pronunciation is *ha-la-payne-yo.*

k- Pronounced like **"KAH"**
l- Pronounced like the letter **"L"** and **"A"** *put together (As in the city in California I think you all have heard of..... LA)*
ll- The double ll sound is probably most commonly known by gringos in the word "tortilla." This letter sounds like the English sound **"ya"**. For example, the word llamar is pronounced (YA-MAR).
m- Pronounced like the letter **"M"** and **"A"** put together (M,A)
n- Pronounced like **"N"** and **"A"** put together (N,A)
ñ - Pronounced like the letter **"N"** and the word **"YAAY"** put together. (N-YAAY)
o- Pronounced like the letter **"O"** (as in *"Oh* My")
p- Pronounced like the English word **"PAY"** (As in I have to *pay* my bill.)
q- Pronounced **"KUWW"**
r- Pronounced like the word **"AIR"** and the letter **"A"** put together (AIR, A)
rr- In Spanish the rr is *trilled*. What is trilled you ask? It is when you roll your tongue so that it rolls into the top of your upper mouth, at which time you should feel a vibration. Yikes, you say, there is an exercise to pronounce a Spanish letter? Yes, but don't worry, *you won't break out in a sweat during this exercise.* My Spanish teacher in high school (shout out to Mrs. Rauch) taught the class an exercise

to practice "trilling" the rr's. It has been 17 years since this class lesson but the "rr" trilling hasn't changed!

Erre con erre cigarro. (Pronounced AIR-RAY/CONE/AIR-RAY/SEE-GAR-RO)

Erre con erre barril. (Pronounced AIR-RAY/CONE/AIR-RAY/BAR-REEL)

Rápido ruedan las ruedas (Pronounced RAP-E-DOE/RUE-A-DON/ LAS/RUE-A-DUS)

Sobre los rieles del ferrocarril (SO-BREY/LOS/RE-L-ACE/DEL/ FAIR-ROH-CAR-REAL)

The closest **English equivalent** to this sound is the way the tongue forms when saying words that start with a **"BL"**, **such** as **blast, blare, blonde**. Also, the double rr in words has a much longer duration, giving a difference between such words as *pero* (but) (Pronounced PEAR-O) and *perro* (dog) (Pronounced PEAR-ROW).

s- Pronounced like the letter **"S"** and **"A"** put together (like the sound of the word *"essay"*)
t- Pronounced like the word **"TAY"** (*Think of Buckwheat from* **The Little Rascals**® *who pronounced the word okay as* **"Otay")**
u- Pronounced **"EWWW"** (As in EWWW that stinks)
v- Pronounced **"EWWW"** **"VAY"**
w- Can be pronounced **"DOE-BLAY-EWW"** and **"DOE-BLAY-VAY"**
x- Pronounced like the letter **"A"** plus **"KEYS"** (but say these two sounds fast together so it flows)
y- Pronounced like the letter **"E"** along with **"GREE-A-GA"** (*EGRIEGA*)
z - Pronounced **"SAY"** **"TUH"**

Okay so now you should have a little understanding as to how the individual letters sound in the Spanish alphabet. My advice to you is to review each letter many times because the pronunciation of these letters give you the basis of not only how each one in its own right is pronounced BUT it gives you the basis to begin forming words and pronouncing them CORRECTLY.

SPANISH WORDS ARE PRONOUNCED EXACTLY HOW THEY ARE SPELLED!!!!!

When starting to learn the pronunciation of words, start out pronouncing the words slowly and then eventually say them faster. When you say the word fast, it will sound closer to the words real pronunciation.

Practice Makes Perfect (La práctica hace la perfección)

A good way to get the hang of these sounds is to practice spelling out your name. Pretend that you are putting your name on a waiting list at a busy restaurant in a Spanish speaking country and the hostess does not understand you when you say your name. You have to spell it for her. I will use my name as an example, (which is not easily understood by native Spanish speakers), so I have to spell it out a lot.

Ejemplo)

Erin - spelled out in Spanish:

E - A
R - "AIR" "A"
I - E
N - "N" "A"

Ejemplo:

Tom

T- TAY
O - OH
M - "M" "A"

Práctica! Now try your name and refer to the way each letter is pronounced in the Spanish alphabet (from above).

When learning these letter and sounds, remember that they are not the same as English and you should learn these sounds so that you can pronounce words correctly!!!! It isn't necessary to be perfect or native in your pronunciation, however it is a good idea to practice pronouncing words as clearly and closely as possible.

A great way to learn Spanish pronunciation is to listen to people speaking Spanish! Listening, whether on the television, radio, or in person, can provide a great first hand insight!

 Remember, there is a big difference in the sound between a jalapeño *and a* **gelapeno!!!!**

¡Cultura!

Don Quixote- **Don Quixote** (Pronounced DON-KEY-HOE-TAY) fully titled ***The Ingenious Gentleman Don Quixote of La Mancha*** is a novel written by Spanish author Miguel de Cervantes. Published in two volumes a decade apart (in 1605 and 1615), *Don Quixote* is considered the most influential work of literature from the Spanish Golden Age in the Spanish literary canon. As a founding work of modern Western literature, and one of the earliest canonical novels, it regularly appears high on lists of the greatest works of fiction ever published. (http://en.m.wikipedia.org/wiki/Don_Quixote_1605.gif)

CAPÍTULO TRES (CHAPTER 3)

Just a numbers game

 In reality, even if you have lived in the most secluded city or town in North America, chances are you have heard at least one number spoken in Spanish. There is even a game from Mattel® (http://en.wikipedia.org/wiki/Mattel) that I grew up with, as I am sure many of you did, called, **Uno** (http://en.wikipedia.org/wiki/Uno (card game), which means **1** in Spanish. (However, I didn't realize that until I actually took Spanish). My point is that there are many common Spanish words that we hear or see every day that you might not have realized you already knew!

My best advice for learning numbers is to really think simply and to try and memorize them in patterns. After #15, the numbers get pretty simple to put together because they consist of patterns.

Okay, we have mastered #1, uno. Let's proceed with the rest of the numbers.

0- **cero** (Pronounced SER-O)
1- **uno** (Pronounced EWW-NO) (as in, "*eww no* I do not like that kind of food")
2- **dos** (Pronounced DOSE, (as in a *dose* of medicine)
3- **tres** (pronounced TRACE) (as in can you *trace* the outline of the shape)
4- **cuatro** (pronounced KWA-TRO)
5- **cinco** (pronounced SINK + O)
6- **seis** (Pronounced SACE)
7- **siete** (Pronounced SEE-ET-A)
8- **ocho** (Pronounced OH-CHO)

9- **nueve** (Pronounced NEW-A-VAY)

10- **diez** (Pronounced DEE-ACE)

11- **once** (Pronounced OWN-SAY) (as in you *own* your own business and you *say* what you think")

12- **doce** (Pronounced DOE-SAY) (*doe* like the deer)

13- **trece** (Pronounced TRE- SAY)

14- **catorce** (Pronounced KA- TOUR-SAY)

15- **quince** (Pronounced KEEN-SAY) (keen as in, he is *keen* on her)

PATTERN In Spanish, the numbers 16 through to 19 are actually contractions. The Gringa Way is to teach it as a simple math problem. I, who am not a math person, still find the following numbers easy. The only catch is that these numbers are written differently.

16- **diez y seis** (word for 10 and for 6) (Pronounced DEE-ACE/E/SACE). Written form is **dieciséis**

17- **diez y siete** (word for 10 and for 7) (Pronounced DEE-ACE/E/SEE-ET-A). Written form is **diecisiete**

18- **diez y ocho** (word for 10 and for 8) (Pronounced DEE-ACE/E/OH-CHO).Written form is **dieciocho**

19- **diez y nueve** (word for 10 and for 9) (Pronounced DEE-ACE/E/NEW-A-VAY). Written from is **diecinueve**

Here is where it gets a little easier and is just repetition:

PATTERN From 20-29

20- **Veinte** (The "vein" is pronounced like the English word VEIN + TAY)

 The only catch here is that **veinte** = 20 becomes veinti (**VEIN-TEE**) when combined with the numbers 1-9.

WATCH how it happens:

21- **veintiuno** (VEIN-TEE-EWW-NO)

22- **veintidós** (VEIN-TEE-DOSE)

23- **veintitrés** (VEIN-TEE-TRACE)

24- **venticuatro** (VEIN-TEE-KWA-TRO)
25- **veinticinco** (VEIN-TEE-SINK-O)
26- **ventiséis** (VEIN-TEE-SACE)
27- **ventisiete** (VEIN-TEE-SEE-ET-A)
28- **ventiocho** (VEIN-TEE-OH-CHO)
29- **ventinueve** (VEIN-TEE-NEW-A-VAY)

Numbers between 30 and 39

You just need to add **"y uno" "y dos" "y tres" "y cuatro,"** etc.

The **"y"** in Spanish translates to **"and"** in English

30- **Treinta** (Pronounced like the English word "TRAIN" and "TA" (Trainta)
31- **treinta y uno** (Basically saying 30 and 1= 31) (TRAIN-TA/E/ EWW-NO)
32- **treinta y dos** (30 and 2= 32) (TRAIN-TA/E/DOSE)
33- **treinta y tres** (30 and 3= 33) (TRAIN-TA/E/TRACE)
34- **treinta y cuatro** (30 and 4= 34) (TRAIN-TA/E/KWA-TRO)
35- **treinta y cinco** (30 and 5= 35) (TRAIN-TA/E/SINK-O)
36- **treinta y seis** (30 and 6= 36) TRAIN-TA/E/SACE)
37- **treinta y siete** (30 and 7= 37) (TRAIN-TA/E/SEE-ET-A)
38- **treinta y ocho** (30 and 8= 38) (TRAIN-TA/E/OH-CHO)
39- **treinta y nueve** (30 and 9= 39) (TRAIN-TA/E/NEW-A-VAY)

PATTERN – The numbers for 40 through 99 are handled the same way as they are for 30-39

40- **Cuarenta** (KWAR-N-TA)
41- **cuarenta y uno** (40 and 1 = 41) (KWAR-N-TA/E/EWW-NO)
41- **cuarenta y dos** (40 and 2 = 42) (KWAR-N-TA/E/DOSE)
43- **cuarenta y tres** (40 and 3 = 43) (KWAR-N-TA/E/TRACE)
44- **cuarenta y cuatro** (40 and 4 = 44) (KWAR-N-TA/E/KWA-TRO)
45- **cuarenta y cinco** (40 and 5 = 45) (KWAR-N-TA/E/SINK-O)
46- **cuarenta y seis** (40 and 6 = 46) (KWAR-N-TA/E/SACE)
47- **cuarenta y siete** (40 and 7 = 47) (KWAR-N-TA/E/SEE-ET-A)

48- **cuarenta y ocho** (40 and 8 = 48) (KWAR-N-TA/E/OH-CHO)
49- **cuarenta y nueve** (40 and 9 = 49) (KWAR-N-TA/E/NEW-A-VAY)

50- Cincuenta (SIN-CUEN-TA)
51- **cincuenta y uno** (50 and 1 = 51) (SIN-CUEN-TA/E/EWW-NO)
52- **cincuenta y dos** (50 and 2 = 52) (SIN-CUEN-TA/E/DOSE)
53- **cincuenta y tres** (50 and 3 = 53) (SIN-CUEN-TA/E/TRACE)
54- **cincuenta y cuatro** (50 and 4 = 54) (SIN-CUEN-TA/E/KWA-TRO)
55- **cincuenta y cinco** (50 and 5 = 55) (SIN-CUEN-TA/E/SINK-O)
56- **cincuenta y seis** (50 and 6 = 56) (SIN-CUEN-TA/E/SACE)
57- **cincuenta y siete** (50 and 7 = 57) (SIN-CUEN-TA/E/SEE- ET-A)
58- **cincuenta y ocho** (50 and 8 = 58) (SIN-CUEN-TA/E/OH- CHO)
59- **cincuenta y nueve** (50 and 9 = 59) (SIN-CUEN-TA/E/NEW-A-VAY)

60- Sesenta (SAY-CEN-TA)
61- **sesenta y uno** (60 and 1 = 61) (SAY-CEN-TA/E/EWW-NO)
62- **sesenta y dos** (60 and 2 = 62) (SAY-CEN-TA/E/DOSE)
63- **sesenta y tres** (60 and 3 = 63) (SAY-CEN-TA/E/TRACE)
64- **sesenta y cuatro** (60 and 4 = 64) (SAY-CEN-TA/E/KWA-TRO)
65- **sesenta y cinco** (60 and 5 = 65) (SAY-CEN-TA/E/SINK-O)
66- **sesenta y seis** (60 and 6 = 66) (SAY-CEN-TA/E/SACE)
67- **sesenta y siete** (60 and 7 = 67) (SAY-CEN-TA/E/SEE-ET-A)
68- **sesenta y ocho** (60 and 8 = 68) (SAY-CEN-TA/E/OH-CHO)
69- **sesenta y nueve** (60 and 9 = 69) (SAY-CEN-TA/E/NEW-A-VAY)

70- Setenta (SAY-TEN-TA)
71- **setenta y uno** (70 and 1 = 71) (SAY-TEN-TA/E/EWW-NO)
72- **setenta y dos** (70 and 2 = 72) (SAY-TEN-TA/E/DOSE)
73- **setenta y tres** (70 and 3 = 73) (SAY-TEN-TA/E/TRACE)
74- **setenta y cuatro** (70 and 4 = 74) (SAY-TEN-TA/E/KWA-TRO)
75- **setenta y cinco** (70 and 5 = 75) (SAY-TEN-TA/E/SINK-O)
76- **setenta y seis** (70 and 6 = 76) (SAY-TEN-TA/E/SACE)
77- **setenta y siete** (70 and 7 = 77) (SAY-TEN-TA/E/SEE-ET-A)
78- **setenta y ocho** (70 and 8 = 78) (SAY-TEN-TA/E/OH-CHO)
79- **setenta y nueve** (70 and 9 = 79) (SAY-TEN-TA/E/NEW-A-VAY)

80- Ochenta (OH-CHEN-TA)
81- **ochenta y uno** (80 and 1 = 81) (OH-CHEN-TA/E/EWW-NO)

82- **ochenta y dos** (80 and 2 = 82) (OH-CHEN-TA/E/DOSE)
83- **ochenta y tres** (80 and 3 = 83) (OH-CHEN-TA/E/TRACE)
84- **ochenta y cuatro** (80 and 4 = 84) (OH-CHEN-TA/E/KWA-TRO)
85- **ochenta y cinco** (80 and 5 = 85) (OH-CHEN-TA/E/SINK-O)
86- **ochenta y seis** (80 and 6 = 86) (OH-CHEN-TA/E/SACE)
87- **ochenta y siete** (80 and 7 = 87) (OH-CHEN-TA/E/ SEE-ET-A)
88- **ochenta y ocho** (80 and 8 = 88) (OH-CHEN-TA/E/ OH-CHO)
89- **ochenta y nueve** (80 and 9 = 89) (OH-CHEN-TA/E/NEW-A-VAY)

90- **Noventa** (NO-VEN-TA)
91- **noventa y uno** (90 and 1 = 91) (NO-VEN-TA/E/EWW-NO)
92- **noventa y dos** (90 and 2 = 92) (NO-VEN-TA/E/DOSE)
93- **noventa y tres** (90 and 3 = 93) (NO-VEN-TA/E/TRACE)
94- **noventa y cuatro** (90 and 4 = 94) (NO-VEN-TA/E/KWA-TRO)
95- **noventa y cinco** (90 and 5 = 95) (NO-VEN-TA/E/SINK-O)
96- **noventa y seis** (90 and 6 = 96) (NO-VEN-TA/E/SACE)
97- **noventa y siete** (90 and 7 = 97) (NO-VEN-TA/E/SEE-ET-A)
98- **noventa y ocho** (90 and 8 = 98) (NO-VEN-TA/E/OH-CHO)
99- **noventa y nueve** (90 and 9 = 99) (NO-VEN-TA/E/NEW-A-VAY)

Do you see the pattern? You only have to learn the words for 20, 30, 40, 50, 60, 70, 80, 90 and 1-10 and viola, you can create the rest of the numbers!

100- cien (Pronounced SEE-N)

1,000 - mil (Pronounced like the English word "MEAL")

1,000,000 - un millón (Pronounced OON/ME-YON)

What's your position?

Think of winning a race. You can come in first, second, third, fourth, etc. as your position ranking. The translations for numbers showing a place or position in Spanish are:

first: **primero** (PRE-MARE-O)
second: **segundo** (SAY-GOON-DOE)

third: **tercero** (TEAR-SEAR-O)
fourth: **cuarto** (KWAR-TOE)
fifth: **quinto** (KEEN-TOE)
sixth: **sexto** (SEX-TOE)
seventh: **séptimo** (SEP-TEE-MOE)
eighth: **octavo** (AUK-TAH-VO)
ninth: **noveno** (NO-VEIN-O)
tenth: **décimo** (DESS-E-MOE)

 These types of numbers follow the same gender (**male/ female**) rule as other words, which you will learn later. When used with descriptive words (aka adjectives), these numbers must agree with the word they refer to, **both in number** (one/more than one) and **gender** (masculine/ feminine).

- **el** quin**to** pis**o** (the noun **"piso" is masculine** because it ends in an "o", therefore the usage of **el** and the ending of **"o"** must be used)
- **la** quin**ta** silla (the noun "sill**a**" is feminine because it ends in an "a", therefore the usage of **la** and the ending of **"a"** must be used)

 When **primero** and **tercero** precede a "one man show" word (aka singular masculine noun in grammar language) the final *-o* is dropped.

Ejemplo: el presidente, el estudiante

- el primer presidente (the first president) (instead of el primero presidente)
- el tercer estudiante (the third student) (instead of el tercero estudiante)

Let's do some practice with your numbers. Out loud, I want you to say the following items using the numbers that you just learned.

¿Cuál es tu número de teléfono? What is your telephone number?

305-123-4567 (tres-cero-cinco-uno-dos-tres-cuatro-cinco-seis-siete)
510-450-1782 (cinco-uno-cero-cuatro-cinco-cero-uno-siete-ocho-dos)

¿Cuál es tu número de seguridad social? What is your social security number?

896-54-1985 (ocho-nueve-seis-cinco-cuatro-uno-nueve-ocho-cinco)
245-85-2768 (dos-cuatro-cinco-ocho-cinco-dos-siete-seis-ocho)

¿Cuál es tu código postal? What is your zip code?

33149 (tres-tres-uno-cuatro-nueve)
33130 (tres-tres-uno-tres-cero)

¿Cuál es tu código de área? What is your area code?

305 (tres-cero-cinco)
907 (nueve-cero-siete)
301 (tres-cero-uno)

¿Cuál es tu número de tarjeta de crédito? What is your credit card number?

1234 5678 9802 14 (uno-dos-tres-cuatro-cinco-seis-siete-ocho-nueve-ocho-cero-dos-uno-cuatro)

Okay let's take a deep breath and pause for a second. Just for reinforcement, *take two deep breaths.* Again, it is important to compute what you are reading and not to rush through these important lessons. Do not get overwhelmed!

¡CULTURA!

 **Tortilla Española-** or *Spanish omelet* is a typical Spanish dish consisting of an egg omelet with fried potatoes. It is the most commonly served dish in Spain. Bars and cafés serve it as a *tapa* or appetizer, but it is often served as a light dinner in Spanish homes. It is also called *Tortilla de Patata* or Potato Omelet. When I was living there they were literally serving this in every restaurant I would go to eat at!

Some days feel like months. Season's Greetings.

One important difference to know for *writing purposes* is that **in Spanish, the days of the *week* AND *months ARE NOT CAPITALIZED,*** as they are in English. The days of the week are all **always masculine.**

Let's learn them shall we!

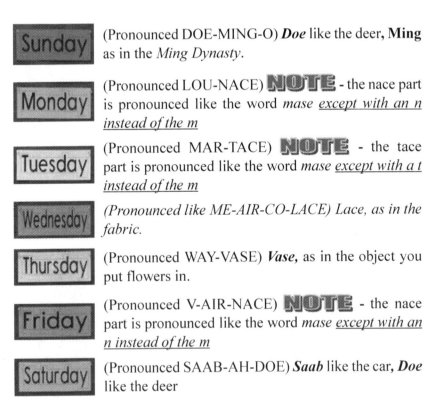

Sunday (Pronounced DOE-MING-O) *Doe* like the deer, **Ming** as in the *Ming Dynasty.*

Monday (Pronounced LOU-NACE) **NOTE** - the nace part is pronounced like the word *mase except with an n instead of the m*

Tuesday (Pronounced MAR-TACE) **NOTE** - the tace part is pronounced like the word *mase except with a t instead of the m*

Wednesday *(Pronounced like ME-AIR-CO-LACE) Lace, as in the fabric.*

Thursday (Pronounced WAY-VASE) *Vase,* as in the object you put flowers in.

Friday (Pronounced V-AIR-NACE) **NOTE** - the nace part is pronounced like the word *mase except with an n instead of the m*

Saturday (Pronounced SAAB-AH-DOE) *Saab* like the car, *Doe* like the deer

Days of the week are usually used with the words **el** *(when talking about one day)* or **los** *(when referring to more than one day) and* it isn't necessary to say that an event happens *on* a certain day as in English. **In Spanish,** the correct way to say *on* a certain day is with el (when referring to one day) or los (when referring to more than one)

Trabajo *los lunes.* (I work *on* Mondays.)
Trabajo *el viernes.* (I work *on* Friday.)

Spanish words that will confuse you at some point

pelar – to peel
pelear – to fight

Phrases associated with the time of days and weeks (frases relacionadas con el tiempo de días y meses)

What day is today? **Qué diá es hoy**? (Pronounced K-DEE-AH/ACE/ OY)

now- **ahora** (Pronounced AH-OAR-AH) (as in "open up and say *ah*")

today- **hoy** (Pronounced OY) (as in the expression "Oy Vey")

yesterday- **ayer** (Pronounced AH-YEAR)

the day before yesterday- **anteayer** (Pronounced AHN-TAY-AH-YEAR)

tonight- **esta noche** (Pronounced ES-STA/NO-CHAY)

last night- **anoche** (Pronounced AH-NO-CHAY)

last year- **el año pasado** (Pronounced L/AHN-YO/PA-SA-DOE)

tomorrow- **mañana** (Pronounced MA-YAHN-UH)

tomorrow morning- **mañana por la mañana** (Pronounced MA-YAHN-UH/POOR/LAH/ MA-YAHN-UH)

the weekend- **el fin de semana** (Pronounced L/FEEN/DAY/ SAY-MAH-NUH)

Los meses (The months)

January February March	enero	febrero	marzo
April May June July	abril	mayo	junio	julio
August September October			
November December	agosto	septiembre	octubre

Helpful Tips — The months are relatively easy to learn due to the fact that all the months **in Spanish,** *(except for January),* **look similar to the months in English.**

January - **enero** (Pronounced A-NEAR-O)

February - **febrero** (Pronounced FAY-BRARE-O) **Feb**ruary-**feb**rero

March - **marzo** (pronounced MAR-ZO) **Mar**ch-**mar**zo

April - **abril** (Pronounced AH-BREEL) Ap**ril**-ab**ril**

May - **mayo** (Pronounced MY-YO) **May**-**may**o

June - **junio** (Pronounced WHO-KNEE-O) **Jun**e-**jun**io

July - **julio** (Pronounced HOOL-E-O) **Jul**y-**jul**io

Helpful Tips — *Julio* is also the name of a boy in Spanish! If you have ever heard this name before then it should make it easy for you to remember July/julio.

August - **agosto** (Pronounced AH-GO-STOW)

September - **septiembre**   <u>Sept</u>ember-<u>sept</u>iembre
(Pronounced SEP-TEE-M-BRAY)

October - octubre   <u>Oct</u>ober-<u>oct</u>ubre
(Pronounced OAK-TU-BRAY)

November - **noviembre**   <u>Nov</u>ember-<u>nov</u>iembre
(Pronounced NO-V-EM-BRAY)

December - **diciembre**   Dec<u>ember</u>-dici<u>embre</u>
(Pronounced D-C-M-BRAY)

What is today's date? ¿Cuál es la fecha de hoy?

I am sure most of you have either heard of or celebrated **"Cinco de Mayo"** before, correct? If the answer is yes, than you are ahead of the game as this stands for **"5th of May"** or "May 5th". The only word you need to add in order to say "the fifth of May" is **el,** which means **the** in Spanish.

```
                    FORMULA

          el + (número) + de + (mes)
          the + (number) + of + (month)
```

Although **English** has the option to give the date in **various ways:**

One way is: (month) + (number) th such as **April 18th, June 5th**

Another way is: (the) + (number) + (of) + (month) such as **the 5th of May** or **the 20th of April**

Spanish only has *ONE* way, as stated above!

The + (number) + of + (month)

el + (quince) + de + (junio) = June 15th
el + (veinte) + de + (marzo) = March 20th
el + (seis) + de + (febrero) = February 6th

el + (cinco) + de + (mayo) = May 5th

Las estaciones (The seasons)

¿Cuál es tu estación favorita? Mi estación favorita es el verano.

(What is your favorite season? My favorite season is summer.)

Summer- <u>el</u> veran<u>o</u> (Pronounced El-VER-AH-NO)

---

* Think of **veran**o as a **veran**da, *somewhere you are able to sit at in the summer!*

Words and phrases associated with summer:

It is hot - **Hace calor** (AH-SAY/KA-LORE)

the sun - **el sol** (L/SOL)

to sunbathe - **tomar el sol** (TOE-MAR/L/SOL)

humidity - **la humedad** (LAH/OO-ME-DAHD)

hurricane - **el huracán** (L/OAR-AH-KAHN)

watermelon - **la sandía** (LAH/SAN-DEE-AH)

picnic - **el picnic** (L/PEEK-NICK)

barbeque - **la barbacoa** (LAH/BAR-BA-CO-AH)

ice cream - **el helado** (L/A-LAH-DOE)

fireworks - **los fuegos artificiales** (LOS/FUAY-GOES/R-TEE-FEES-E-AL-ACE)

the beach - **la playa** (LAH/PLA-YAH)

bathing suit/swim trunks - **el traje de baño** (L/TRA-HAY/DAY/BAHN-YO)

to swim - **nadar** (NAH-DAR)

to tan - **broncearse** (BRON-SAY-R-SAY)

suntan lotion - **el bronceador** (L/BRON-SEE-AH-DOOR)

sunglasses - **las gafas de sol** (LAS/GAF-US/DAY/SOL)

to camp - **acampar** (AH-CAHM-PAR)

Winter - e̲l̲ inviern̲o̲ (Pronounced L/INN/V-AIR-NO)

> *Think of *in*vierno as being the opposite to verano (summer), when you are *inside*!

It is cold - **Hace frío** (AH-SAY/FREE-OH)

snow - **la nieve** (LAH/KNEE-A-VAY)

to snow - **nevar** (NAY-VAR)

snowflake - **el copo de nieve** (L/CO-POE/DAY/KNEE-A-VAY)

snowman - **el muñeco de nieve** (L/MOON-YAY-CO/DAY/KNEE-A-VAY)
hailstorms- **la granizada** (LAH/GRAN-E-SA-DAH)
hail/sleet - **el granizo** (L/GRAN-E-SOW)

snowstorm - **una tormenta de nieve** (OO-NA/TOR-MEN-TA/DAY/KNEE-A-VAY)

a skate - **un patín** (OON/PA-TEEN)

figure skating - **patinaje artístico**
(PA-TEE-NAH-HAY/R-TEE-STEE-CO)

a ski - **un esquí** (OON/S-KEY)

to ski - **esquiar** (S-KEY-R)

Spring - <u>la</u> primaver<u>a</u> (LAH/PRE-MA-VER-AH)

* Think of *pasta primavera* (an Italian-American dish that consists of pasta and fresh vegetables), which I am sure you have seen on a menu at an Italian restaurant. The bright colors of the vegetable medley are used to signify spring.

Easter - **la Pascua** (LAH/PASS-KWA)

flower - **la flor** (LAH/FLOOR)

butterfly - **la mariposa** (LAH/MAR-E-POE-SUH)

rainbow - **el arco iris** (L/R-KO-E-RIS)

Fall - e̲l̲ otoñ<u>o</u> (Pronounced L/OWN-TONE-YO)

> * Think of **otoño** in an abstract way. Since fall proceeds winter, which brings cold weather, think of relating this word to *o to no* (*heat*)

Thanksgiving Day - **Día de Acción de Gracias** (DEE-AH/DAY/ ACK-SEE-OWN/DAY/GRA-SEE-US)

a pumpkin - **una calabaza** (OO-NAH/CAL-AH-BAH-SAH)

turkey - **el pavo** (L/PAH-VO)

leaf - **la hoja** (LA/O-HA)

How is the weather today? ¿Qué tiempo hace hoy? (K/T-M-POE/ AH-SAY/OY)

It is nice weather - **Hace buen tiempo** (AY-SAY/BUANE/T-M-POE)
It is bad weather - **Hace mal tiempo** (AY-SAY/MALL/T-M-POE)

It is = Hace_____

hot	**calor** (KA-LORE)
cold	**frio** (FREE-O)
cool	**fresco** (FRESS-KO)
sunny	**sol** (SOUL)
windy	**viento** (V-N-TOE)

What time is it?

¿Qué hora es? The basic way of telling time in Spanish is to use the word **es**, *for one o'clock* (**only used** for one o'clock) and **son** (*used for all other times*).

es and son translate into **"It is"** in English. Minutes can be stated simply by separating them from the hour using **"y"** (the word for **"and"** in English).

> **es/son** = It is
> **y** = and

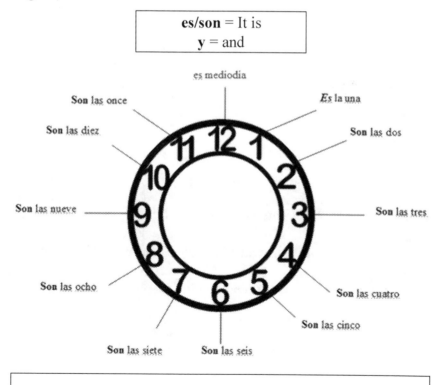

To indicate the *half hour,* use *media.* You have to add the word **"y"** before **media.** It literally translates to **"and a half."**

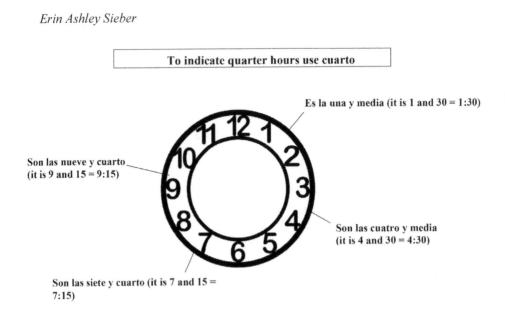

To indicate quarter hours use cuarto

Es la una y media (it is 1 and 30 = 1:30)

Son las nueve y cuarto (it is 9 and 15 = 9:15)

Son las cuatro y media (it is 4 and 30 = 4:30)

Son las siete y cuarto (it is 7 and 15 = 7:15)

Unlike in English, **in Spanish,** it is common to use the **upcoming hour** to tell time during the second half of each hour. You state the number of minutes until the following hour and count back using the word **menos** (Pronounced **MEH-NOS**). *It is basically a math problem so if you are good at math, you should have no problem with this!*

Por ejemplo, if it is **7:55** you would say Ocho *menos* cinco **(literally 8:00-5 minutes = 7:55)**

- It is **12:52** = Es la una **menos** ocho (literally 1:00 - 8 minutes = 12:52)
- It is **4:55** = Son las cinco **menos** cinco.(literally 5:00 - 5 minutes = 4:55)
- It is **8:40** = Son las nueve **menos** veinte. (literally 9:00 - 20 minutes = 8:40)
- It is **7:45** = Son las ocho **menos** cuarto. (literally 8:00 - 15 minutes = 7:45)

Anything pertaining to the time of *day, morning, afternoon* **or** *night* **will have these words in them.**

the day - **el día** (Helpful Tips día starts with **"d"** and so does **d**ay. They also have the exact same amount of letters, three.)

the morning - **la mañana** (Helpful Tips **m**añana starts with **"m"** and so does **m**orning.)

the afternoon - **la tarde** (pronounced TAR-DAY)

the nigh - **la noche** (Helpful Tips **n**oche starts with a **"n"** and so does **n**ight. They also have the exact amount of letters, five!)

Greetings (Saludos)

Once you learn the words for day, morning, afternoon and night, you can make the following greetings just by adding the word "Buenos" for días and "Buenas" for tardes and noches.

Good morning - **Buenos días**

Good afternoon - **Buenas tardes** (used *after noon*)

Good evening, good night (as either a greeting or a farewell) - **Buenas noches** *(used after sunset)*

> When you are in public place, you might hear a native speaker address you, or perhaps of group of people when they walk into a room, by saying only **"Buenas"**. This is a short and very informal way of saying "Buenos días/Buenas tardes/Buenas noches". You can also use "Buenas" yourself if you want to sound more native or can't remember the words for morning, afternoon or night.

To tell a <u>specific time</u> of morning, afternoon or night, you add the word "de" in front

- Son las siete y cuarto **de la mañana**. It's 7:15 a.m. (**in the morning**)

- Son las cuatro menos cinco **de la tarde**. It's 3:55 p.m. (**in the afternoon**)
- Son las ocho y media **de la noche**. It's 8:30 p.m. (**at night**)

To indicate a <u>non specific</u> time of morning, afternoon or night, you add the word "por" in front

- **por la mañana** - the morning (**no specific time**)
- **por la tarde** - the afternoon (**no specific time**)
- **por la noche** - in the evening or night (**no specific time**)

Expresiones relacionadas con el tiempo (Time related expressions):

tomorrow morning - **mañana por la mañana** (MA-YAHN-UH/POOR/ LAH/ MA-YAHN-UH)

the day after tomorrow-**pasado mañana** (PAH-SAH-DOE/ MA-YAHN-UH)

yesterday - **ayer** (AH-YEAR)

last night - **anoche** (AH-NO-CHAY)

the night before last - **la noche anterior** (LAH/NO-CHAY/ AHN-TEAR-E-OAR)

next week - **la semana que viene** (LAH/SAY-MAH-NUH/K/V-N-A)

last week - **la semana pasada** (LAH/ SAY-MAH-NUH/PAH-SAH-DUH)

last year - **el año pasado** (L/AHN-YO/PAH-SAH-DOE)

at noon - **al mediodía** (AL/MEH-DEO-DEE-AH)

at midnight - **a la medianoche** (AH/LAH/MEH-DEA-UH-NO-CHAY)

during the day - **durante el día** (DO-RAHN-TAY/L/D-AH)

on time - **a tiempo** (AH/T-M-POE)

on the dot - **en punto** (N/POON-TOE)

¡CULTURA!

La Plaza Mayor - The Plaza Mayor was built during the Habsburg period and is a central plaza in the city of Madrid, Spain. It is located only a few blocks away from another famous plaza, the Puerta del Sol. The Plaza Mayor is rectangular in shape, measuring 129 by 94 meters, and is surrounded by three-story residential buildings having 237 balconies facing the Plaza. It has a total of nine entranceways. (http://en.wikipedia.org/wiki/Plaza_Mayor,_Madrid)

Capítulo seis (Chapter 6)

The colors of a rainbow

color = **color** (Pronounced CO-LORE)

colors = **colores** (Pronounced CO-LORE-ACE)

What color is it? ¿De qué color es?

> white - **blanco/a** (Pronounced BLAHN-KOH/KA) Such as in the *Casa Blanca* or White House)
>
> black - **negro/a** (Pronounced NEH-GROW/GRA)
>
> blue - **azul** (Pronounced AH-ZOOL) *Note*- I use to have a BLUE fish named Azul, rest his soul!
>
> green - **verde** (Pronounced VER-DAY)
>
> yellow - **amarillo/a** (Pronounced AH-MAH-REE-YO/YA) (*Also a city in Texas*)
>
> orange - **anaranjado/a** (Pronounced AH-NA-RAHN-HA-DOE/DA)
>
> pink - **rosado/a** (Pronounced ROW-SAH-DOE/DA)

red - **rojo/a** (Pronounced ROW-HO/ ROW-HA)

brown - marrón o café (Pronounced MAH-RONE) or (CALF-A)

 Just remember that *coffee (*also translated as *café in Spanish)*, is also brown*!*

gray - **gris** (Pronounced like the English word ***Grease***) *As in the movie*

gold - **dorado/a** (Pronounced DOE-RAH-DOE/DAH)

purple - **morado/a** (Pronounced MORE-AH-DOE/DAH). Can also you *púrpura* (Pronounced POOR-POOR-AH) for the color purple

 In most cases, names of colors come **after the words they describe**, **not before** as in English.

Ejemplo: Una casa **blanca** (A **white** house)

- Tengo **un** coche **amarillo**. (I have **a yellow** car.) *Car* is masculine so "o" is used.
- Tienes **una** flor **amarilla**. (You have **a yellow** flower.) *Flower* is feminine so "a" is used.
- Tiene **dos** coches **amarillos**. (He has **two yellow** cars.) More than one car. (masculine)
- Tenemos **ocho** flores **amarillas**. (We have **eight yellow** flowers.) More than one flower. (feminine)

 Note that there are two different versions of the colors used, where applicable. One version is with an **"o"** and one is with an **"a"**. This is because when you are describing **anything** (person, place, thing, etc) by color, you have to use the masculine (man)

or feminine (female) Spanish ending. Typically, masculine endings have an "o" and feminine endings have an "a". In addition, if the (person, place, thing, etc) you are describing is just one (singular) or more than one (plural) you have to use their appropriate word endings. Don't worry about this right now, as you will learn soon enough. Then you can come re-visit this chapter and apply the rules!

At this point, we have covered all items contained in **Phase 1** of The Gringa Way:

- The alphabet
- Numbers
- Days of the week
- Months
- Seasons
- Telling Time
- Colors

At this juncture, you should take a few weeks and review the sections each day. Why? Well I am sure you are thinking "Oh my gosh" and feeling a little overwhelmed, right? This is why absorption and understanding of the material is of utmost importance. You have to learn in phases, making sure you reach full development of each phase and the material covered before you move on to the rest!

Up until this point you have learned basic words and concepts. These words and concepts have introduced you to the language. Try and master the above lessons. It will give you more confidence if you can learn the beginning steps and lessons first. The key is to learn the basics so you can move on to each level with ease instead of frustration. If you learn all the aspects of the basics, then you will already have a lot of Spanish under your belt. Trust me, it gets a wee bit trickier from here so give yourself a head start and master the above lessons!

The Gringa Way Phase 2

Spanish is very literal BUT cannot be translated literally from English to Spanish.

Instead you need to think in a more abstract way when you want to translate your English thoughts into Spanish.

Here are some ejemplos to show you how Spanish is literal.

* **¿A quien le toca?**- Who's turn is it (literally translates as, *who does it touch?*)
* **vale la pena**- It is worth it (literally translates as, *it is worth the shame/punishment*)
* **echar la culpa**- to blame (literally translates as, *to throw the blame*)
* **Tengo calor** - I am hot (literally translates as, *I have heat*)
* **¿Cómo te llamas?**- What is your name? (literally translates as, *How do you call yourself?*)
* **¿Cuántos años tienes?**- How old are you? (literally translates as, *How many years do you have?*)
* **hacer la maleta** - to pack (literally translates as, *to make your suitcase*)
* **cama matrimonial** - double bed (literally translates as, *marital bed*)
* **guardaespaldas** - bodyguard (literally translates as, *back guardar*)
* **tocar la puerta** - knock on the door (literally translates as, *to touch the door*)
* **antepasados** - ancestors (literally translates as, *those who passed before*)
* **estado civil** - marital state (literally translates as, *civil state/status*)
* **anteojos** - glasses (literally translates to, *before eyes*)

Spanish words that will confuse you at some point
casada/o - married
cansada/o - tired

Capítulo Siete (Chapter 7)

"Stress" (el estrés)

Ah yes, I am sure that is what you have right now attempting to learn a foreign language but in this chapter, stress is referring to emphasis placed on Spanish words. Let me be the first to admit that stress (which can be shown with written **accent marks**) was the first lesson and quiz I had on my second day of Spanish language in 9th grade high school. Had I not gone on to master the Spanish language, I would have been embarrassed to admit the following: *I failed my stress test!* Yes, it was the first Spanish quiz I ever took and I failed it. Why do I tell you this? I want you to understand that at first glance or first go around, you might not be the Spanish master you want to be but fear not my fearless students, you will eventually get it!

"Stress" (estrés) refers to the loudness of a syllable. In Spanish, one syllable of a word usually is louder than the others. Stress is important because it can completely change the meaning of a word.

Por ejemplo, the following words are spelled identically, except for the location of the stressed syllable (which changes the meaning of the words):

papá - father
papa - potato

Another key aspect is knowing which syllable should be stressed, which also changes the pronunciation of the word. *Very important for speaking purposes!*

Fortunately, in Spanish, there are rules for stress and these rules are pretty straightforward. In fact, there are only three basic rules that cover nearly every word:

1. If a word ends in a *vowel* (**a, e, i, o, u**), *n* or *s*, the stress is on the next to last syllable.

   Por ejemplo: esta (Pronounced S-TAH) and *zapatos* **(Pronounced ZAH-PAH-**TOES) **all have their accent on** *the next to last syllable.*

2. Words that end in other letters have the stress on the last syllable.

   Por ejemplo: *hotel* **(**Pronounced OH-**TELL***)* **and** *hablar* (Pronounced AH-**BLAR) have the accent on the final syllable.**

3. If a word isn't pronounced according to the above two rules, an accent is placed over the vowel of the syllable that gets the stress.

   Por ejemplo: *común* (Pronounced CO-**MOON),** *lápiz* (Pronounced **LAH-**PIECE**),** and *ojalá* (Pronounced O-HA-**LAH) all have the stress on the indicated syllable.**

 Personal names and place names of foreign origin usually are written without accents (unless accents are used in the originating language).

 The accent marks are used to distinguish two similar words with the same spelling **when written** and they don't affect pronunciation (because the marks are already on a syllable that is being stressed).

The following lists are words that are spelled the same but that have different meanings with and without accent marks.

Without Accent Marks	With Accent Marks
como - as	**¿cómo?**- how?
de - of, from	**dé** - you give (dar/to give)
el - the	**él** - he
mas - but	**más** - more

45

mi - my	**mí** - me
que - than, that	**¿qué?** - what?
si - if, whether	**sí** - yes
solo - alone	**sólo** - only
te - you	**té** - tea
tu - your	**tú** - you

 This stress lesson is really a memorizing exercise and if you are able to understand and learn these rules in the beginning it should just come more naturally to you when speaking or writing.

INTERVENTION!

Put down anything you might be picking up besides this book and replace it with this book, at least until you grasp the basics and start to understand the language!!!!! I still do this all the time. In fact, there are many days where, as much as I want to listen to my favorite radio station or watch my favorite TV shows in English, I often opt for a Spanish radio station or Spanish television instead. Why is this? Because even though I am not in the learning stage of the language, I still need to maintain it. I still need to hear the language being spoken to be consistent. Because it is my second language, I still need to work at retaining the language. The best thing for you to do is to do the same thing. In the beginning you need to do more of it. Replace listening to your favorite English radio station either on the way to and from school, work, the grocery store, doctor, etc with a Spanish radio station. Pick at least one way of your car ride in which you are going to listen to a Spanish radio station. Same with television. If you are not near a TV or radio station, download one to your IPAD and listen to Spanish as much as can! *Trust me, it will help you tremendously and speed the process of learning along!* If you are not living in a Spanish speaking country, this is the second best way to be immersed and hear Spanish being spoken!

Spanish words that will confuse you at some point
el cuento – the story
la cuenta – the account, the check

CAPÍTULO OCHO (CHAPTER 8)

Spanish you already know but might not think you know!

Have you ever been to a Mexican restaurant here in the States? Have you ever ordered food from Taco Bell™ (http://en.wikipedia.org/wiki/Taco_Bell) or ever heard of a state by the name of Florida? Then chances are you have already spoken and know some Spanish! Was it hard for you to place your order at the Mexican restaurant? Probably not. Why? Because when you go out to eat in a Mexican restaurant, it is second nature to you. You might not realize that by ordering "salsa" or your "enchilada" that you are speaking Spanish. Granted, you might not be saying "Me gustaría tener una enchilada por favor" (I would like to have an enchilada please) but by merely saying 'taco", or burrito", you are speaking Spanish! Now you might not know what the words really mean but the whole point here is that you may know more Spanish than you think you do and you learned these words without any frustration or any inhibitions, right? That is the way you need to move forward learning Spanish. *People get tripped up on learning things when they actually become conscious that they are learning or studying*! They look at it as a daunting task or one that is going to require effort. Like I mentioned earlier, it is all in your mind and your outlook!

Let's go over some words you might already know:

sí - yes

no - This is actually how you say no in Spanish!

Hola - Hi

margarita - How can we not know this one! *(I like mine on the rocks with no salt.)*

cerveza - beer (comes in a can, bottle, draft and keg)

taco - I would like a chicken one please with extra queso (cheese).

enchilada - Great menu item that usually comes with chicken, beef or shrimp

burrito - Bigger than an enchilada

chimichanga - A deep-fried burrito that is popular in Southwestern U.S. cuisine

tortilla - A tortilla is daily bread in Mexico – a flat, pancake-like disc made from masa harina or wheat flour and baked on a griddle

salsa - As in chips and salsa

tequila - Needs no explanation!

fiesta - This word for *party* is used a lot. In fact, Lionel Richie uses it his song "All Night

Long" We're going to party Liming, *fiesta,* forever (http://en.wikipedia. org/wiki/All_Night_Long_(All_Night)

piñata - Well known for being used at kids birthday parties where candy flies out when you hit it

amigo - As in the movie ¡**Three Amigos**!(http://en.wikipedia.org/wiki/ Three_Amigos)

siesta - As in I am tired and going to take a siesta/nap (note- siestas are taken seriously in Spanish speaking countries. When I was living in Spain, the city would literally shut down for two hours in the afternoon for siestas!)

Los Angeles - Meaning ("The Angels") is the most populous city in California

Florida - You are probably a little stumped with this one. Didn't know this was a Spanish word? This comes from the discovery in 1513 by Spanish explorer Juan Ponce de León – who named it *La Florida* ("Flowery Land") upon landing there during the Easter season. (Pronounced FLOR-E-DUH in Spanish)

Puerto Rico - The US owned island (meaning rich port or harbor)

Livin' **La Vida Loca** - (Living the Crazy Life") - is a song by Puerto Rican singer Ricky Martin. You probably didn't even think about this one as it went so mainstream in the US you probably forgot that you were actually signing or listening to some Spanish when this song came on! (Source: http://en.wikipedia.org/wiki/Livin'_la_Vida_Loca)

Yo quiero Taco Bell - If you live in the US and haven't been living under a rock, then chances are you have heard this very popular slogan! This slogan means "I want Taco Bell™" In Spanish. This slogan is a completely grammatically correct sentence in Spanish. If you have ever said this slogan, than congrats, you have already spoken a complete sentence in Spanish! (http://en.wikipedia.org/wiki/Taco_bell)

Okay, so that was easy right? You already know some Spanish! Good, now hopefully you start telling yourself that:

✓ Yes, you do in fact know some Spanish
✓ Yes, you can do this

Now try and think of more words that you may know that are not listed here. You could be quite surprised at how much Spanish you already know!

¡CULTURAl

Debajo el reloj de la Plaza Mayor (under the clock of the Plaza Mayor)

The clock of the Plaza Mayor is the most famous meeting point within the city of **Salamanca, Spain**. It's the central point of the town and it's known by everybody. A lot of young and old people stay there throughout the day to have lunch, to take a walk, to have dinner or to go out at night. It is a busy focal point of Salamanca and there are always people just relaxing or waiting under the clock.

Capítulo nueve (Chapter 9)

Mirror Images and Fake ones too!

The grammatical term you would be taught in a classroom is **cognates.** Yikes, a technical term! Don't freak out and close the book. The Gringa Way refers to this lesson as **Mirror Images** (imágenes espejadas). This is because I don't want you getting hung up on technical words which can be daunting, and two, this lesson is about words **that exist in two languages that are spelled exactly or almost exactly the same way and have the same meaning,** *hence the Mirror Image name.* Easy, right? This is one aspect of learning Spanish that will help make it easier for you to learn vocabulary.

You can simply use your knowledge of English vocabulary and apply the rules that determine the spelling change between the two languages. How is this you ask? The Spanish language has evolved from Latin over the last two thousand years. The English language, although not as closely related to Latin as Spanish, borrows thousands of words from Latin, many of which use the same words that Spanish uses. In addition, English and Spanish have borrowed many words from Classical Greek. This results in thousands of Mirrored Image words between English and Spanish, acting as a bridge to connect words from the English language to the Spanish language. *This is where it helps you!*

While some of the words with a common origin in Latin have different meanings in the two languages (these are called **false cognates**), 30-40% of all words in English have a related word in Spanish and the vast majority of them, 90% or more, have a similar enough meaning to be useful to you as you learn Spanish. Wow think about that for a minute, if 30-40% of all words in English have a Spanish counterpart, this means you start out knowing 30-40% of Spanish words right out of the gate!

The following are some words that are spelled and mean exactly the same in English and Spanish but are just pronounced differently in Spanish. Now as you will note, when you are reading, the words will appear to look the same and are easy to guess what the word means. Even though the words written have the same spelling and meaning (minus the false cognates) speaking the words is more challenging because the pronunciation is different.

Let's learn some! (*¡Aprendamos algunos!*)

agenda (Pronounced AH-HEN-DUH but spelled the same as in English)

amnesia (Pronounced AHM-NEH-SEE-AH)

anorexia (Pronounced ANN-OR-EX-E-AH)

armadillo (Pronounced R-MAH-DEE-YO) like the animal

bar (Pronounced the same as in English)

base (Pronounced BAH-SAY)

cable (Pronounced COBB-LAY) Cobb as in the salad, lay as I am going to lay down

canal (Pronounced KA-NAL)

capital (Pronounced CAP-E-TALL) cap as in a baseball cap, E as in the English letter and tall, as in you are very tall!

casino (Pronounced CAH-SEE-NO) Pronounced the same as in English

chance (Pronounced CHAN-SAY)

chocolate (Pronounced CHO-KO-LAH-TAY)

control (Pronounced CONE-TROLL) Cone as in an ice cream cone, troll as in the mythological creature

diploma (Pronounced DEE-PLO-MA)

gas (Pronounced the same as in English)

hotel (Pronounced O-TELL) **This is because, as you learned earlier, the "h" is silent in Spanish**

idea (Pronounced E-DAY-AH)

Okay now let's learn some simple rules regarding how to easily make an English word into Spanish:

> The majority of words ending in **TION** *in English* end in **CION** *in Spanish*. Basically, you replace the TION with CION to make it a Spanish word.

invitation = **invitación** (Pronounced EEN-V-TA-SEE-OWN)

relation = **relación** (Pronounced RAY-LAH-SEE-OWN)

education = **educación** (Pronounced EH-DUE-KAH-SEE-OWN)

occupation = **occupación** (Pronounced OAK-U-PA-SEE-OWN)

vision = **visión** (Pronounced VEE-SEE-OWN)

> The majority of English words ending in **OR** have a Spanish word that *is identical*. Here are some ejemplos:

director = **director** (Pronounced DEE-RECK-TOUR)

factor = **factor** (Pronounced FACT-TOUR)

actor = **actor** (Pronounced a little differently AK-TOUR but spelled the same as in English)

color = **color** (Pronounced CO-LURE, (as in fish lure)

doctor = **doctor** (Pronounced DOCK-TOUR)

motor = **motor** (Pronounced MOE-TOUR)

error = **error** (Pronounced A-ROAR)

> The majority of English words ending in **AL** have a Spanish word that *is identical*

musical = **musical** (Pronounced MOO-SEE-CALL)

animal = **animal** (Pronounced AH-KNEE-MALL)

capital = **capital** (Pronounced CAH-PEE-TALL)

legal = **legal** (Pronounced LAY-GAL)

natural = **natural** (Pronounced NAH-TO-RAWL)

local = **local** (Pronounced LOW-CALL)

usual = **usual** (Pronounced OO-SUE-ALL)

> The majority of English words ending in **BLE** *have* a Spanish word that *is identical*.

honorable = **honorable** (Pronounced O-NOR-AH-BLAY)

visible = **visible** (Pronounced V-C-BLAY)

> The majority of words ending in **TY** *in English* end in **DAD** *in Spanish.*
> Basically, you replace the TY with DAD to make it a Spanish word

variety = **variedad** (Pronounced VAR-E-A-DAD)

property = **propiedad** (Pronounced PRO-PRE-A-DAD)

city = **ciudad** (Pronounced C-OO-DAD)

university = **universidad** (Pronounced EWW-KNEE-VERSE-E-DAD)

society = **sociedad** (Pronounced SO-C-A-DAD)

> The majority of words ending in **IST** *in English* end in **ISTA** *in Spanish.* Basically, you replace the IST with ISTA to make it a Spanish word.

artist = **artista** (Pronounced R-TEE-STA)

novelist = **novelista** (Pronounced NO-VEH-LEE-STA)

feminist = **feminista** (Pronounced FAY-ME-KNEE-STA)

tourist = **turista** (Pronounced TOUR-E-STA)

conformist = **conformista** (Pronounced CONE-FOR-ME-STA)

> The majority of words ending in **NCE** *in English* end in **NCIA** *Spanish.*
> Basically, you replace the NCE with NCIA to make it a Spanish word.

obedience = **obediencia** (O-BAY-D-N-SEE-UH)

importance = **importancia** (EEM-POOR-TAHN-C-AH)

distance = **distancia** (DEE-STAHN-C-AH)

incidence = **incidencia** (EEN-C-DEN-C-AH)

coincidence = **coincidencia** (CO-EEN-C-DEN-C-AH)

> The majority of words ending in **IC** *in English* end in **ICO** *in Spanish.* Basically, you replace the IC with ICO to make it a Spanish word.

plastic = **plástico** (Pronounced PLAS-TEE-COH)

traffic = **tráfico** (Pronounced TRA-FEE-COH)

magic = **magico** (Pronounced MAH-HE-COH)

> The majority of words ending in **ARY** *in English* end in **ARIO** *in Spanish.* Basically, you replace the ARY with ARIO to make it a Spanish word.

itinerary = **itinerario** (E-TIN-EH-RAH-REE-OH)

imaginary = **imaginario** (E-MAH-HE-NAH-REE-OH)

See how may words you know that you didn't think you knew in Spanish? **These words are basically free vocabulary!!!!!!!** A lot of times when I am trying to think or remember a word in Spanish and I say what the word is in English in Spanish, I think I am inventing the word because it sounds too easy that an English word would be the same in Spanish. However, the majority of the time I am correct, because you can take many English words, change the pronunciation and voila..... you have a Spanish word!

False Mirror Images

Have you ever heard the expression, **"You can't judge a book by its cover"?** Well in terms of the following words, this expression holds true. There are many words in Spanish that when read, look as if they resemble an English word. A lot of times people will see a Spanish word and think that just because it looks like the English word, that it has the same meaning. That is not always the case. Be very careful with the following words **as the way they look does not translate to their meaning!** As you will see below, words that you think would be translated one way really are not! Instead you should wrap your mind around the differences and the concept of the word(s) and meanings.

 Embarazada is NOT embarrassed. The way you say embarrassed in Spanish is *avergonzado/a*. Any guess what the real meaning of embarazada is? **It means *pregnant!*** Yikes, that is a big difference in meanings! And yes, you will feel embarrassed if you use the word embarazada instead of avergonzado/a!!!!!! **This is probably the most widely used false mirror image** and in my opinion the biggest difference in meaning to how the word appears and what the actual meaning is!

Here are ejemplos of more *false mirror image words* to be careful of:

Spanish word	English meaning	English word for:	Spanish translation
actual (Pronounced AK-TWO-AWL)	current, present	**actual**	efectivo, verdadero
aplicar (Pronounced AP-LEE-CAR)	to apply, to attach	**to apply (for a job)**	solicitar
educado (Pronounced ED-EWW-KA-DOE)	polite, well mannered	**educated**	culto
compromiso (Pronounced KOM-PRO-ME-ZO)	commitment	**compromise**	un arreglo
constipacion (Pronounced CONE-STE-PA-SEE-OWN)	cold, illness	**constipation**	estreñimiento
carpeta (Pronounced CAR-PAY-TUH)	folder, file	**carpet**	la alfombra

campo (CAM-POE)	country, field	**camp**	el campamento
enviar (Pronounced N-V-R)	to send	**to envy**	envidiar
éxito (Pronounced EX–E-TOE)	success	**exit**	la salida
collar (PRONOUNCED COH-YAR)	necklace	**collar**	el cuello
contestar (Pronounced CONE-TES-TAR)	to answer, to reply	**to contest**	disputar
fábrica (Pronounced FAH-BREE-KA)	factory	**fabric**	la tela/ el tejido
atender (Pronounced AH-TEN-DEER)	to take care of	**to attend**	asistir
introducir (Pronounced INN-TRO-DUE-SEAR)	to introduce (a topic or an object), to insert	**to introduce**	presentar
largo (Pronounced LAR-GOH)	long	**large**	grande
lectura (Pronounced LEC-TOUR-AH)	reading	**lecture**	la conferencia
molestar (Pronounced MO-LESS-TAR)	to annoy, to bother	**to molest**	abusar sexualmente
librería (Pronounced LEE-BREH-REE-AH)	bookstore	**library**	la bibloteca

mayor (Pronounced MY-YOUR)	greater, older	**mayor**	el alcalde
pinchar (Pronounced PEEN-CHAR)	to puncture	**to pinch**	pellizcar
realizar (Pronounced REY-AH-LEE-SAR)	to carry out (in terms of completing)	**to realize**	darse cuenta de
red (Pronounced same as in English)	network	**red**	rojo
recordar (Pronounced REY-CORE-DAR)	to remember	**to record**	grabar
ropa (Pronounced ROW-PAH)	clothes	**rope**	una cuerda
sopa (Pronounced SO-PAH)	soup	**soap**	el jabón
sensible (Pronounced SEN-SEE-BLEH)	sensitive	**sensible**	razonable, prudente
nudo (Pronounced NEW-DOE)	knot, joint	**nude**	desnudo
pie (Pronounced PEE-A)	foot	**pie**	el pastel
tabla (Pronounced TAH-BLAH)	board, plank, table top	**table**	una mesa

advertencia (Pronounced AHD-VEER-TEN-SEE-AH)	warning	**advertisement**	un anuncio
arena (Pronounced AH-REY-NAH)	sand	**arena**	anfiteatro
asistencia (Pronounced AH-SEES-TEN-SEE-AH)	attendance (can also mean assistance	**assistance**	ayuda, auxilio
bachillerato (Pronounced BATCH-E-YEAR-AH-TOE)	high school diploma	**bachelor**	un soltero
bufete (Pronounced BOO-FET-A)	A desk, or a law firm	**buffet**	una comida buffet

Para diversión! For fun!

The first song I learned from Spanish natives made me a hit with them. When I was living in Spain "mis tios" as they call friends in Spain, taught me a song. It is really a children's song but hey, you got to start somewhere! It goes a little something like this:

Tengo una vaca lechera. *(I have a milk cow.)*

No es una vaca cualquiera. *(It isn't just any cow.)*
Me da leche condensada. *(She gives me condensed milk.)*
¡Ay! ¡Qué vaca tan salada!! *(Wow! What a salty cow!)*
tolón, tolón,
tolón, tolón.

Even though the meaning of this song is about a milk giving cow, (I know it is corny), as a gringo (a) singing this song to natives, you will be a hit. I walked around the streets of Spain singing it and instantly made friends!!!!!!

> **Spanish words that will confuse you at some point**
> **pero** - but
> **perro**(a) - dog

Capítulo diez (Chapter 10)

It more than just size!

The easy part about Spanish is that you can just add a different ending to a lot of words in order make a new one! As you just learned from the cognates, you can build your vocabulary just by changing the ending of a word. There are couple different endings (proper term being suffix/ es) that denote a specific meaning when added to an already existing Spanish word. I use these word endings a lot because they are easy to tack onto a word and it changes the meaning of a word with just a different ending! Think of it this way; you have double the ways of saying a word and only have to memorize one way in order to create the second! **These suffixes are mostly just in *spoken communication.***

"ito" "cito" "ita" "cita"

Just because something is diminutive in Spanish doesn't necessarily mean it's small. The most common Spanish suffixes are **-ito and -cito** along with their feminine equivalents, **-ita and -cita** *and most* often translated to the English word **"little"**. However, even though the translation of "little" has to do with *size,* the meaning of little is also used to make a *word less harsh* or to *indicate affection.* Por ejemplo, in English when a mother says to her 6 foot tall adult son "my little boy" (mi hij**ito**) she is saying it not literally but rather in an affectionate way.

The English counterpart endings are **"-ie"** or **"-y"** of words such as **"jammies"** (for pajamas) or **"doggy."**

Did you realize?

If you have ever ordered the Gordita Baja, Gordita Supreme or Gordita Nacho Cheese off of a Taco Bell™ menu, then you have already used one of these endings! Bet you didn't know that when you ordered it! Gord**ito** is the **"little"** form of gordo, meaning fat. Basically, gordita translates into **little fatty**.

¡CULTURA! A lot of Latin's call each other gordito/a! You will hear them say, ¡Oye gordito/a! (Hey fatty)! I know, I know, if someone called us fatso or little fatty in English we would be offended but in Spanish they use this as a term of endearment (more or less).

The way you add on these endings is easy. You simply drop the final vowel or letter and add -*ito* or -*ita*, -*cito* or -*cita* to it.

* perro = dog/ **perrito** = puppy or little dog
* casa = house / **casita** = little house, cottage

When you are speaking to your friends you can take your friends name add these endings. It makes it seems like you are talking to them in a more affectionate way. (Keep in mind that if it is a girl, you will add *ita, cita* and if it is a boy, you add *ito, cito*)

* Melissa = Meliss**ita**
* Juan = Juan**ito**
* mamá (mom) = mam**ita**
* amigo (friend) = amigu**ito/ita**

Here are additional ways the meaning of a word changes when you add these suffixes to a word in Spanish:

To indicate something is charming or endearing:

* mi abuela (my grandmother) mi abue**lita** (my dear grandmother)
* papá (dad) pap**ito** (daddy)
* pajaro (bird) pajar**ito** (birdy)

To provide a slight degree of difference, especially with descriptive words:

* ahora (now) ahor**ita** (right now)
* cerca (close) cerqu**ita** (very near)
* gordo (fat) gord**ito** (chubby)

To give a friendly tone to a sentence:

* un momento (a moment) un momen**tito**, por favor. (Just a moment, please.)
* ¡Despacio! (Slow!) ¡Despac**ito**! (Easy does it!)

"ería"

Spanish words that end in "eria" denote some sort of business (shops). If you have ever traveled to a Spanish speaking country, I am sure you have seen many of these words, as every city contains at least one of the below list. If you have not traveled to a Spanish country but plan on it at some point (recommended) then you can keep an eye out for these business names!

Cafetería = Coffee shop (from the Spanish word *cafe*, meaning coffee)

Carnicería = Butcher shop (the Spanish word *carne*, meaning meat)

Cervecería = Brewery, Bar (from the Spanish word *cerveza*, meaning beer)

Confitería = Candy store (from the Spanish verb, *confitar*, meaning to confect candy)

Floristería = Flower shop (from the Spanish word, *flor*, meaning flower)

Heladería = Ice cream palor (from the Spanish word *helado*, meaning ice cream)

Joyería = Jewelry shop (from the Spanish word *joya*, meaning jewel)

Lavandería = Laundry mat (from the Spanish word *lavar*, to wash)

Librería = Bookstore (from the Spanish word *libro*, meaning book)

Panadería = Bakery (from the Spanish word *pan*, meaning bread)

Papelería = Stationery store (from the Spanish word *papel*, meaning paper)

Pastelería = Pastry shop (from the Spanish word *pastel*, meaning pastry)

Peluquería = Hair salon (from the Spanish word *pelo*, meaning hair)

Pescadería = Fish shop (from the Spanish word *pescado*, meaning fish)

Pizzería = Pizza parlor (from the Spanish word *pizza*, meaning pizza)

Sombrerería = Hat shop (from the Spanish word *sombrero*, meaning hat)

Zapatería = Shoe store (from the Spanish word *zapato,* meaning shoe)

At this point we have covered all items contained in **Phase 2** of The Gringa Way:

- Liternal aspects of Spanish
- Word stress
- Spanish you already know
- Mirror Images
- Suffixes

Remember, it is important to feel comfortable, not frustrated and not rushed with the information you have learned thus far. If you feel you still don't have a good grasp on the above chapters, then you should go back and review each chapter again.

Spanish words that will confuse you at some point
el polvo - the dust
el pavo - the turkey

The Gringa Way Phase 3

Capítulo once (Chapter 11)

¿Masculino o femenino? Masculine or feminine?

All words in Spanish are either *masculine* **or** *feminine.* Repeat this again! **All words in Spanish are either masculine or feminine. There are no** *hermaphrodite* **words!** I know, right now you are saying, *what?* The grammatical term for a masculine/feminine word that you would learn in a traditional Spanish class is called an "article" but as far as you are concerned, an article refers to a piece of clothing, or something you read in a newspaper or magazine, *right?*

Let me make it very simple. In Spanish, everything has a **gender specification**, from a chair, to a table, to a glass of water, etc. This is a lot different from English where everything is basically defined with the word **"the"**. When I first heard this in Spanish class many moons ago, I had a hard time grasping the concept that a table or a chair or anything for that matter (other than being a boy or girl) had a gender specification. I had to come to grips with this because it is very essential when speaking Spanish. The gender specification in Spanish is one of the most confusing concepts for people learning the language to grasp.

So what word do you use with a masculine word and what word do you use with a feminine word?

Masculine words use **"el"** in front of the word

Feminine words use **"la"** in front of the word

What does **el** and **la** mean? It means **"the"** in Spanish!

> Generally speaking **masculine** nouns end in "o" and **feminine** nouns end in "a"
>
> **el** is used in front of "o" ending words and **la** is used in front of "a" ending words

The language is very specific. Take the name of this book for ejemplo. Gringa (feminine ending) is used instead of Gringo (masculine ending) because I, the author, am a woman.

* <u>La</u> Gring<u>a</u> - if you are a women
* <u>El</u> Gring<u>o</u> - if you are a man

Another ejemplo is one that was already presented to you in the chapter "Spanish You Already Know"

"Livin' La Vida Loca" This sentence is a great ejemplo as "La vida loca" is all in agreement with the feminine endings: <u>La</u> vid<u>a</u> loc<u>a</u> (**la vida is feminine and ends in an "a", NOT a masculine "o"**) That is why it is **NOT** la vida loco.

Even though there is a standard rule that states that words that end in "a" are usually **feminine** and words that end in "o" are **masculine**, there are also additional endings that are categorized as either feminine or masculine.

Let's take a look:

Feminine ♀	**Masculine** ♂
-a	-o
-d	-or
-cion	-j
-sion	-r
-dad	-ma

-tad	-n
-tud	-r
-sis	-s
-ez	-i
-z	-u

By the way *some* do not follow the **o/masculine** and **a/feminine** rule: YIKES! **This is where the powerful tool of memorization comes into play!**

la mano - the hand (try to remember the phrase "**la** mano arriba" (the raised hand)

la foto - the photo (comes from the word fotograf**ía**, hence the femininity)

la moto - the motorcycle (comes from the word motocicle**ta**, hence the femininity)

la disco - the discotheque (comes from the word discotec**a**, hence the femininity)

el día - the day (try to remember the holiday *el dia de acción de gracias* (Thanksgiving)

el agua - the water (try to remember this phrase: frio frio como **el agua** del rio)

el mapa - the map

el programa - the program, the show

el tema - the topic, the theme

el sistema - the system (**NOTE** tema, contained in sis**tema,** is masculine as well, so just memorize one or the other and you will know both!)

el problema - the problem

el clima- the weather

el telegrama - the telegram

el idioma - the language

el sofá - the sofa

el planeta - the planet

el poema - the poem

el poeta - the poet

la radio - the radio

el aroma- aroma

el plasma- plasma

el panorama- panorama, outlook

There are a few additional exceptions to the above words but these are a good starting point for you. In addition, there are a couple other tricks in regards to the masculine/feminine topic. These are easy and if you learn these you won't have to think that hard when speaking, because you will already know the masculine/feminine compliment to a word!

- **Masculine words that end in a "consonant" often have a corresponding feminine form that ends in -a.**

el doctor/la doctora

el señor/la señora

el profesor/la profesora

- **Many words that denote "living things" have both a masculine and a feminine form**

  el perro/la perra (male dog/female dog)

  el abuelo/la abuela (grandfather/grandmother)

  el chico/la chica (male boy/female girl)

  el gato/la gata (male cat/female cat)

- *Some* **words that refer to people use the same form for both masculine and feminine. These nouns indicate gender by the determiner** *(el or la).*

  el pianista/ la pianista

  el artista/ la artista

  el estudiante/la estudiante

It is imperative that you know if a word is masculine or feminine and use el and la properly because you will not be saying a word correctly if you don't use el and la correctly. Por ejemplo, there is no such thing as "el silla" so if you say this; you are **not** saying "the chair" correctly. You have to learn and remember that the correct way to say "the chair" is "la silla" (again if you now the word silla you know it ends in an "a" you can assume it must be feminine, *because it is not on the list of exceptions*)

FOOD for Thought

Did you know that a native Spanish speaker, unless they actually studied the Spanish language grammatically in depth, does not know that there are masculine/feminine words? If you ask a native Spanish speaker why the chair is feminine (la silla) and not el sillo they will almost always tell you they don't know or didn't realize it was feminine, because that is just the way they grew up speaking the language. They just learned it as la silla!

More than one!

Okay so the above mentioned masculine/feminine words were singular, meaning just one. What happens when there is more than one (person, place or thing)?

The word for **"the"** becomes:

> **el = los** (masculine singular/ masculine plural)
> **la = las** (feminine singular/ feminine plural)

 In regards to masculine and feminine correlations in Spanish **"It's a man's world"** (*do not get mad at me* girls). I am merely using *this expression for learning purposes! As long as a group of creatures has at least one male member, a word takes the masculine format and corresponding masculine word ending, regardless of how many women are involved.*

Por ejemplo: There could be four male dogs and two female dogs together but if you are going to refer to the <u>group of dogs</u>, you have to say **"los perros"** and not **"las"**, **due to the fact there is at least one male member in the group.**

Let's take a look!

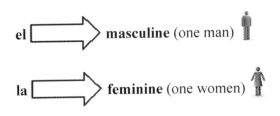

el ⟹ **masculine** (one man)

la ⟹ **feminine** (one women)

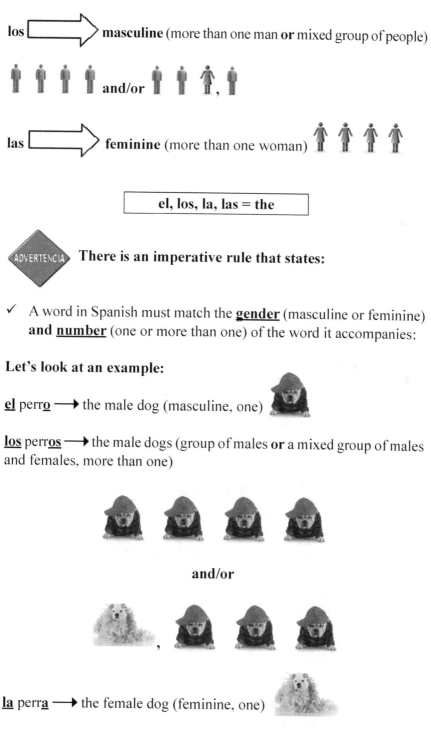

los ⟹ **masculine** (more than one man **or** mixed group of people)

and/or ,

las ⟹ **feminine** (more than one woman)

> **el, los, la, las = the**

ADVERTENCIA **There is an imperative rule that states:**

✓ A word in Spanish must match the **gender** (masculine or feminine) and **number** (one or more than one) of the word it accompanies:

Let's look at an example:

el per**ro** ⟶ the male dog (masculine, one)

los per**ros** ⟶ the male dogs (group of males **or** a mixed group of males and females, more than one)

and/or

,

la perr**a** ⟶ the female dog (feminine, one)

las perr**as** ⟶ the female dogs (group of only females, more than one)

In addition, there are three guidelines to make a word plural:

If a person, place or thing *(aka noun in grammar world)* **ends in:**

- a vowel (a,e,i,o,u), **add "s"** to the word: puerta/puerta**s** (door/doors), libro/libro**s** (book/books)
- a letter (not a vowel), **add "es"** to the word: profesor/profesor**es** (teacher/teachers)
- **-z,** you just change it to a **"c" and add "es"**: luz/lu**ces** (light/lights), lápiz/lápi**ces** (pencil/pencils)

> **"Soy"** *plus* **el/la = I am the**

> **"Eres"** *plus* **el/la = You are the**

> **"Es"** *plus* **el//la = It is the**

> **"Somos"** *plus* **los/las = We are the**

> **"Son"** *plus* **los/las = They are the**

(All you have to do is add the word you are talking about that corresponds to either el/la)

Ejemplos: I am the teacher **(Soy la** profesora)

You are the teacher **(Eres el** profesor)

It is the way it is **(Es la manera** que es)

We are the owners **(Somos los** dueños)

They are the actors (Ellos son los actores)

Spanish words that will confuse you at some point
la fuente - the fountain
el puente - the bridge

You just leaned the masculine and feminine words for "the" in Spanish and how you have to use them accordingly. Now let's learn a set of words that also have a masculine/feminine and one/more than one form when used in front of Spanish words.

---

un, una = a, an
unos, unas = some, a few

The 4 forms are:

un ⟹ **a** (masculine, one)

una ⟹ **a** (feminine, one)

unos ⟹ **some, a few** (masculine **or** mixed group, more than one)

unas ⟹ **some, a few** (feminine, more than one)

Let's look at an example:

<u>**un**</u> perr<u>o</u> ⟶ **a** male dog (masculine, one)

<u>**una**</u> perr<u>a</u> ⟶ **a** female dog (feminine, one)

<u>**unos**</u> perr<u>os</u> ⟶ **some/a few** male dogs (group of males **or** a mixed group of males and females, more than one)

and/or

<u>**unas**</u> perr<u>as</u> **some/a few** female dogs (group of only females, more than one)

The Spanish verb **"es"** plus **un/una** = **It is a**
(All you have to do is add the word you are talking about that corresponds to either un/una)

Ejemplos: **It is a** way to live - **Es una** manera de vivir

It is a good car - **Es un** buen coche

It is a faster way to do things - **Es una** forma más rapida de hacer las cosas

Let's Look At the Comparisons Again!

<u>el</u> perr<u>o</u> - **the** male dog/ **<u>un</u>** perro- **a** male dog

<u>la</u> perr<u>a</u> - **the** female dog/ **un<u>a</u>** perr<u>a</u> - **a** female dog

<u>los</u> perr<u>os</u> - **the** male dogs/ **<u>unos</u>** perr<u>os</u> - **some** male dogs (more than one male **or** mixed group with males and females)

<u>las</u> perr<u>as</u> - **the** female dogs/ **un<u>as</u>** perr<u>as</u> - **some** female dogs (more than one female)

¡CULTURA!

Did you really know?

Cinco de Mayo (Spanish for "fifth of May") is a holiday held on **May 5th.** I am sure many of you reading this book have either celebrated a Cinco de Mayo once or twice or at least heard of it. It is celebrated nationwide in the United States and regionally in Mexico, primarily in the state of Puebla, where the holiday is called **El Día de la Batalla de Puebla** (The day of the Battle of Puebla). The date is observed in the United States as a celebration of Mexican heritage and pride, and to commemorate the cause of freedom and democracy during the first years of the American Civil War. In the state of Puebla, the date is observed to commemorate the Mexican army's unlikely victory over French forces at the Battle of Puebla on May 5, 1862, under the leadership of General Ignacio Zaragoza Seguín. Contrary to widespread popular belief, **Cinco de Mayo *IS NOT Mexico's Independece Day.*** Mexico Independence Day is actually celebrated on September 16th. (Source: http://en.wikipedia. org/wiki/Cinco de Mayo)

Hey *YOU*, Yeah *YOU* heard me, I am talking to *YOU*, What's it to *YOU*?

tú = you (when speaking to someone informally, such as friends and family; who you know well) **¿Cómo estás?**

utsted = you (when speaking to someone politely or formally, such as an elder, a boss, teacher) **¿Cómo está?**

ustedes = you (when speaking to more than one person, can translate as "you all") **¿Cómo están?**

vosotros = you (informal but mostly only used in Spain and one or two countries in Central America) **¿ Cómo estáis?**

Almost any form from a doctor's office, school, employer, etc. will be written in the **usted** form. This is because they do not know you on a personal level and therefore use the formal form of you (usted).

I would recommend not using the vosotros form (no offense to vosotros or the people who use it). I have found in my Spanish career and real world interactions that only people from Spain and Nicaragua use this format. For learning purposes, it is easier for you to stick with the other "you" formats. I mention it above as a reference so you are aware that it exists.

Capítulo doce (Chapter 12)

"The Who"

The grammatical term is **subject pronoun** but The Gringa Way refers to it as **"The Who"** Why? **Because it answers the question, *"who"*!** Now some people might find these words sometimes unnecessary, but they really do provide emphasis and clarity when speaking and they are used a lot! (I actually like using them because I think it makes you sound more versed in the language, so I use them whenever I can fit them into a sentence!

In English, there is eight of *"The Who"* and in Spanish there are only five. They are:

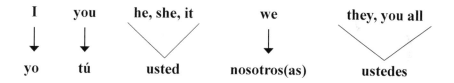

I	you	he, she, it	we	they, you all
yo	tú	usted	nosotros(as)	ustedes

The difference between the English "The Who" and the Spanish "The Who" is that in Spanish they must agree with the gender of its subject (here is that frustrating masculine/feminine thing again). You have already learned about that, so this should be a breeze for you!

Let's take a look at them again:

- **I = yo** (Pronounced the same way you say **"yo"** in English)

- **you** = **tú** (Pronounced TWO)

- **he, she, you = él, ella and usted (formal)**
  él (Pronounced like the English letter "L")
  ella (Pronounced A-YA)
  usted (EWW-STEAD)

> **The Gringa Way** - The easiest way to remember *usted* is by the beginning of the word (**u**sted = you)

- **we = nosotr<u>os</u>, nosotr<u>as</u>** (Take notice of both of these forms....look familiar?) We just finished learning masculine/feminine agreement. The nosotr<u>os</u> (Pronounced NO-SO-TROSE) form is used when referring to men and the nosotr<u>as</u> (Pronounced NO-SO-TRASS) form is used when referring to women.

- **you all = ustedes** (Pronounced EWW-STEAD-ACE) **(Take notice!** usted = you, **u**stedes = you all)

- **they = ell<u>os</u>** (Pronounced A-YOS), **ell<u>as</u>** (Pronounced A-YUS)

> **The Gringa Way**
>
> ellos and ellas is just the plural for of él (ellos) and ella (ellas)
>
> The word for he is **él** so just add **los** to this word without accent mark (el + los = ellos) when referring to "**they the men**"
>
> The word for she is **ella**, so just add and **s** to this word (ella + s = ellas) when referring to "**they, the women**"

Ejemplo: If you want to say "They will go to school today" (and you are talking about your two children who are *girls*), you would say "*ellas* van a ir a la escuela hoy". If you were talking about two **boys**, you would say "*ellos* van a ir a la escuela hoy."

> **NOTE** Generally, there is not a corresponding word for "it" when used as the subject of a sentence. When you need to say "**it**" in a sentence or phrase, it is understood by using "**es**"
>
> **Ejemplo:** What color *is* your house? *Es* blanca ("It is" white)

Let's look at *how & when* you can and would use the "The Who" in a sentence, weather spoken or written.

"The Who" are in **boldface**:

To report something:

* Te amo, gritó **él**. También te amo, respondió **ella**. "I love you," **he** yelled. "I love you too," **she** responded.

(Here you can see the importance of using the "The Who". Without it, you wouldn't be clear of who was telling who they loved them!)

To clarify something:

* Mi sobrina y su esposo son inteligentes. **Ella** es abogada, y **él** es doctor. My niece and her husband are intelligent. **She** is a lawyer, and **he** is a doctor.

* **Tú, ella** y **yo** vamos al cine. **You, she** and **I** are going to the movies. (Using "The Who" here is clarifying *who is going to the movies*.)

Ejemplo - I didn't know that you didn't know = No sabía que no sabía
This sentence could be very confusing to figure out who you are talking to and about if you looked at this sentence. However, if you use "The Who", it will clear it up:
Yo no sabía que **usted** no sabía = I didn't know that **you** didn't know

---

Giving a command

* *Hazlo* **tú**. (**You** do it.) In a command situation, adding the corresponding ("The Who") often has a similar effect to its use in English.

When descriptive words start a sentence

* *A menudo* va ella al centro. (She *often* goes downtown.)

In Summary (en resumen)

The English "The Who" The Spanish "The Who"

I	yo
you	tú
he, she, it	él, ella, usted
we	nosotros (as)
they, you all	ellos, ellas, ustedes

Capítulo trece (Chapter 13)

Where do I direct my object?

Okay, so now that you have mastered how to use "The Who" to indicate who is doing something, you are now going to learn "to whom" you should direct your object.

English:

me, you, him, her, you, it, us, them

You use these every day and it is probably so subconscious to you that you don't ever look at it abstractly as to why....to answer the question, *to whom*? The good news is, that in Spanish, they work the same way. The purpose is to replace the name(s) of object(s)/people in a sentence.

The **Spanish counterparts:**

me - **me** (Pronounced MAY)
you - **te** (Pronounced TAY)
him, her, you, it - **lo/la** (Pronounced LOW/LAH)
us - **nos** (Pronounced as NOS)
them, you all - **los/las** (Pronounced as LOHS/LAHS)

Ejemplos)

- Will you call **me**? ¿**Me** llamará usted? (Answers the question, *who will you call?)*
- I love **you** - **Te** quiero. (Answers the question, *who do you love?*)
- She gave **us** the money - Ella **nos** dio el dinero. (Refers to *who she gave the money to).*

> **NOTE** As you can see, the "who" words are used instead of using names and making sentences longer.

The usage of "lo"

"it"

"Lo" is a very interesting word, as not only is it use to define "he" but **lo** can also be used as an object determiner to refer to something abstract, to an unnamed activity or situation, or to a previous statement. In this cast it translates into the English word **"it"**:

- I want <u>it</u> - **Lo quiero** (action word)
- They can't do <u>it</u> - No pueden hacer<u>**lo**</u>.
- I don't understand <u>it</u> - No **lo** comprendo
- <u>It</u> isnt. No **lo** es.

lo que = what, that which

- No entiendo **lo que** me dijiste - I don't understand **what** you told me.
- No puedo decidir **lo que** es mejor - I can't decide **that which** is better.

"Lo" is also used in various phrases so all you have to do is memorize the phrases and you will add more words to your vocabulary! Here are some commonly used phrases:

- **a lo largo de** (AH/LOW/LAR-GO/DAY) - **throughout**
- **por lo tanto** (POOR/LOW/TAHN-TOE) - **as a result**
- **saberlo todo** (SUH-BEAR-LOW/TOE-DOE) - **to know it all**
- **por lo general** (POOR/LOW/HEN-AIR-ALL) - **generally**
- **por lo menos** (POOR/LOW/MAY-NOSE) - **at least**
- **por lo pronto** (POOR/LOW/PRONE-TOE) - **for now**
- **a lo mejor** (AH/LOW/MAY-HORE) - **probably**

In Summary (en resume)

| English "The Who" | Spanish "The Who" |

English "The Who"	Spanish "The Who"
me	me
you	te
him, her, you, it	lo/la
us	nos
them	los/las

Spanish words that will confuse you at some point

el cuadro - the painting
la cuadra - the block (of buildings)

Capítulo catorce (Chapter 14)

"Possession is nine-tenths the law"

What is possession? The old adage says that possession is nine-tenths law but we don't need to get that in depth to understand what is yours and what is mine. The concept of possession should be a fairly simple one to wrap your mind around. It entails the same meaning in Spanish as in English, just with different words. Basically, it means you or someone else, posses something.

These English possessive words might look familiar:

mine, yours, his, hers, its, ours, theirs

The function of using possessive words is to replace the name of the owner and object so you don't have to keep repeating a person's name. In Spanish, the possessive word that answers the question ("The Who") comes immediately after the conjugated action word. Let's learn the Spanish counterparts!

Only one person	More than one person
mine - mi<u>o</u>, mi<u>a</u>, mi<u>os</u>, mi<u>as</u>	
yours - tuy<u>o</u>, tuy<u>a</u>, tuy<u>os</u>, tuy<u>as</u>	**ours** - nuestr<u>o</u>, nuestr<u>a</u>, nuestr<u>os</u>, nuestr<u>as</u>
his, hers, yours, its - suy<u>o</u>, suy<u>a</u>, suy<u>os</u>, suy<u>as</u>	**theirs, yours** - suy<u>o</u>(s), suy<u>a</u>(s)

Please remember that these words must match the word they represent in both **number** and **gender**. Remember that the

o, os, and **a, as** are the gender indicators; **o/os** for **male(s)**, **a/as** for **female(s)**.

Unlike the equivalent words in English, the Spanish possessive words are usually preceded by the determining words **el, la, los or las.**

mío, mía, míos, mías = mine

* Su madre y **la mía** no pueden bailar = Your mother and **mine** can't dance.
* No me gustan los coches rojos. **El mío** es verde = I don't like red cars. **Mine** is green.

tuyo, tuya, tuyos, tuyas = yours (one/ informal)

* Este cuaderno no es **mío.** Es **tuyo.** = This notebook isn't **mine.** It's **yours.**
* ¿Dónde está mi mochila? **La tuya** está aquí. = Where is my backpack? **Yours** is here.

suyo, suya, suyos, suyas = his, hers, yours (one or more than one/ formal), its, theirs

* Mis calcetines son blancos. **Los suyos** son azules. = My socks are white. **His/hers/yours/theirs** are blue.

nuestro, nuestra, nuestros, nuestras = ours

* Este sofá es **nuestro.** = This sofa is **ours.**
* ¿Le gusta su casa? No me gusta **la nuestra.** = Do you like your house? I don't like **ours.**

At this point we have covered all items contained in **Phase 3** of The Gringa Way:

- Questions
- Describing
- Por vs. Para
- Ser vs. Estar

Remember, it is important to feel comfortable, not frustrated and not rushed with the information you have learned thus far.

¡CuLTuRA¡

If you have ever been to Miami, Florida, you might have noticed that you had a hard time finding someone to speak English to (this is an over exaggeration....but not really). This is because the city is more than 60% percent Latin. That is correct. The gringos in Miami, FL are a minority. There are more people of Latin decent than there is non-Hispanic. I love this about Miami and that is the reason I moved there. I didn't want to hear any English and wanted to practice my Spanish. It worked out great! The story behind Miami's transformation into a Hispanic majority county is a forty year old story. The Miami area has come to be defined by the large population of Cuban-Americans that have emigrated to the city of Miami and Miami-Dade County in great numbers over the years. The growth of the Cuban population has been increased due to the shifting nature of Cuban-American political tensions. After Fidel Castro assumed power in Cuba in 1959, many Cubans emigrated in protest of the communist regime. Many of these immigrants chose Miami as their new home. As a result, Miami gained certain magnetism to future Cuban immigrants wishing to settle in a land other than Cuba. Cuba's upper-middle class departed *en masse* (in masses) once Castro began confiscating their material wealth. There is a great neighborhood in Miami called **Little Havanna**, (named after the capital of Cuba, Havana) and was named this in the 60's as the concentration of Cubans in the area grew sharply. It lies just west of Downtown Miami and stretches for several miles and is famous for being the cultural and political capital of Cuban Americans. The neighborhood is a center of the Cuban exile community. (http://en.wikipedia.org/wiki/LittleHavana)

The Gringa Way Phase 4

Capítulo quince (Chapter 15)

Being Interrogated

in·ter·rog·a·tive

Adjective: Having or conveying the force of a question

Noun: A word used in questions, such as how or what

As the name interrogative suggests, interrogative words are those that **are used almost exclusively in *questions.*** Their function is to set up a question for which the answer is the name of a person or thing. The same is true for both English and Spanish. (***Good news***). You already know the English ones so now all you have to do is learn the Spanish corresponding ones.

In English we change the order of the subject and person in order to make a question.

They have eaten (*this is a statement*) = Have they eaten? (*this is a question*)

In Spanish there is no change in the word order

You know that someone is asking a question because there is a *change in intonation at the end of the sentence.*

In written Spanish there are question marks both at the beginning and at the end of the question.

Ejemplos: ¿Tienes fuego? Do you have a light?

¿Va Pedro al mercado? Is Pedro going to the market?

¿Roberto tiene que ir al banco? Does Roberto have to go to the bank?

¿Juan se va mañana? Is Juan leaving tomorrow?

How do I ask a question in Spanish? ¿Cómo hago una pregunta en español ❓

There are really two ways that you can ask a question in Spanish. It is important to learn how to ask a question, as you might have a lot of them. After all, you can't get an answer if you don't ask a question.

One way: With question words.

The most common English question words:

Who? What? Where? When? How? Why?

The Spanish counterparts:

¿ Quién/Quiénes? ¿Qué? ¿Dónde ? ¿Cuándo? ¿Cómo? ¿Por qué?

• **Who**

¿Quién? (Pronounced KEY-N) (when speaking of one person)

¿Quiénes? (Pronounced KEY-N-ACE) (when speaking of more than one person)

Who works there? Josefina works there -¿**Quien** (one person) trabaja allí? *Josefina* trabaja allí.

Who lives in the big house? Pedro and Jose live there - ¿Quién vive el la casa grande? *Pedro* y *Jose* viven allí.

- **What**

¿Qué?(Pronounced "K")

What do you want to do today?¿**Qué** quieres hacer hoy?

What are you saying? ¿**Qué** dices?

*Please take time to learn this one! It is used in many expressions in Spanish and is one of those words that you will come to use very often.

- **Where?**

¿Dónde ? (Pronounced DONE-DAY)

Where is the bathroom? ¿**Dónde** está el baño?

Where are you? ¿**Dónde** estás?

- **When?**

¿Cuándo? (Pronounced KWAN-DOE)

When are you going to arrive? ¿**Cuándo** vas a llegar?

When is your anniversary? ¿**Cuándo** es su aniversario?

- **How?**

¿Cómo? (Pronounced KO-MOE)

How did you get here? ¿**Cómo** llegaste aquí?

How do you write it? ¿**Cómo** se escribe?

- **Why?**

  ¿Por qué? (Pronounced POOR-K)

  Why didn't you say so? - ¿**Por qué** no lo dijiste?

  Why not? - ¿**Por qué** no?

 Notice that the "question words" have accents on them (for writing purposes).

 There are many more "question words" that you can learn but these are the basics that will give you a good starting tool.

¿Yes/no?/ ¿verdad? Questions

Another way to make a question is using no or verdad. **In English,** you would say: *correct?* or *right?* to insinuate a question. **In Spanish,** you just add the word *"verdad"* or *"no"* to the end of the question and use a raised intonation.

> verdad = true

Ejemplo:

- You live in Spain, right? ¿Vives en España, ¿*verdad*? or ¿Vives en España, ¿*no*?
- You went to movies, correct? ¿Fuiste a la película, ¿*verdad*?

 In written Spanish, you only place the question marks around the portion of the sentence that is a question.

Capítulo dieciséis (Chapter 16)

Which one do you want?

There are words that exist in both English and Spanish that point to specific things. The technical word for them is Demonstrative Pronouns but..... *yikes,* that word is much too profound for such simple words. Don't bog yourself down with the technical word; just remember **"which one do you want"** ¿**Cuál quieres?**

this, that, these, those

If you were alive in the 20th Century, you might remember a popular song from a rapper named Snoop Dogg. Here is a verse from **"Nuthin But a G Thang"** (**http://en.wikipedia.org/wiki/Nuthin' but a 'G' Thang**) to show you the usage of these words in English:

> It's like **this** and like **that** and like **this** and uh
> It's like **that** and like **this** and like **that** and uh
> It's like **this** and like **that** and like **this** and uh

These specific words in English serve basically the same purpose in Spanish. They act as an equivalent of **"this," "that," "these"** or **"those"** in English. The key difference, is that in Spanish, there are masculine/feminine endings that need to be used depending to what or to whom you are referring.

(*one*) masculine/feminine	(*more than one*) masculine/ feminine
this - **éste/esta** (S-TAY/ S-TAH)	these - **estos/estas** (S-TOES/ S-TUS)
that - **ése** /**esa** (S-A/S-AH)	those - **esos/esas** (S-O's/S-UH's)
that over there - **aquél /aquella** (UH-KELL/UH-K-YA)	those over there - **aquellos/aquéllas** (UH-K-YOZ/UH-K-YUS)

Ejemplos:

- Yo probé muchos sombreros. Voy a comprar *éste*.
  I tried on many hats. I'm going to buy ***this one***.

(**This *one*** refers to the ***sombrero*** you are going to buy). Sombrero (hat) is ***masculine***, which is why you use *"éste."*

- Me probé muchas camisas. Voy a comprar *ésta*.
  I tried on many shirts. I'm going to buy ***this one***.

(***This one*** refers to the ***camisas*** you tried on). Camisa (shirt) is *feminine*, which is why you use *"ésta"*.

- Quiero esta flor. No quiero *ésa*.
  I want this flower. I don't want ***that one***.

(***That one*** refers to *flor)*. Flor (flower) is *feminine*, which is why you use *"ésa."*

- Me gustan esas casas. No me gustan *aquéllas*.
  I like those houses. I don't like ***those over there***.

(***Those over there*** refer to the ***casas)***. Casas (houses) is *feminine*, which is why you use *"aquéllas."*

 It is important to continue to keep in mind that when talking about one or more than one, it is referring to anything. It could be glasses of water, a car, dresses in the window of a store, a person, etc.

¡Cultura!

If you have ever heard an English speaking person from England, Australia, Ireland or any other native English speaking country, you have probably picked up on the fact that the **lieu** is not the same word that we U.S. of A. natives use for the bathroom and **the Barbie** is not a barbeque in the U.S. of A. It is in fact a popular children's doll. My point to this? Spanish words can vary from different Spanish speaking countries, just like that of English words. Words that mean something in one country, may mean something different in another country.

Por ejemplo, when I was living in Spain, and I was shopping for jeans, I would say to me friends "Necesito ir y comprar **vaqueros**" (I need to go and buy **jeans**). However, when I arrived to Miami and I was speaking with a Cuban friend of mine and I said this same thing, she turned to me and gave me a puzzled look, vaqueros she said? I said, yes, vaqueros..... jeans. I told her that I know I am saying it right because I just learned it in Spain and was using this word all of the time when talking about jeans. She kept saying that it was not what that word meant. Basically, to sum up this conversation, we looked up this word up in the dictionary and yes, vaqueros can mean jeans. To her, in the Cuban dialect, and in may other Spanish speaking countries, vaqueros means cowboys, not jeans. The same thing has happened with the word for "juice". In Spain, you use the word **zumo** for juice, such as *zumo de naranja* (orange juice). However, when I arrived to Miami and I was speaking with a person from Latin America and I happened to mention that I wanted a zuma de naranja, the person looked at me and really didn't understand me. They then said, zumo? I said, yes zumo. I had to explain to them I wanted juice. They told me I was mistaken and that **jugo** is the word for juice. I politley informed them that zumo means juice. After a small debate, I grabed a Spanish dictionary and showed them that in fact, zumo is a word for juice! The point here? Even people who are native Spanish speakers don't always know the words (that mean the same thing) used in other Spanish speaking countries. And because you are a gringo, they automatically think that you do not know what you are talking about. You must show them that you do! You can actually teach Spanish to a native speaker if you learn the different words!

Here are some other differences in vocabulary between Spain & Latin America:

English	(Spain) Spanish	Latin American Spanish
car	el coche	el carro
avocado	el aguacate	la palta
to get angry	enfadarse	enojarse
computer	el ordenador	la computadora
peach	melocotón	durazno
potato	la patata	la papa
bus	la wawa	el autobús
friend	tío/tía *(anywhere else it means "uncle/aunt")	amigo/amiga
mushroom	el champiñón	el hongo
apartment	el piso	el apartamento
bathroom	el baño	el servicio
cool, great	chulo	chévere
eyeglasses	las gafas	los anteojos
lunch	la comida	el almuerzo
pretty	bonito/a	lindo/a
bean	la judía	el frijol
shrimp	la gamba	el camarón
to throw out	tirar	botar
juice	jugo	zumo

Spanish words that will confuse you at some point
el collar – the necklace
el cuello – the neck

"SP" *words in Spanish*

Living in Miami, the Latin capital of the US as I like to refer to it as, you hear a lot of Latin people pronounce English "sp" words with an "e" in front of them. It is not just a coincidence that they pronounce English "sp" words this way. So why do they?

This is because, in general, Spanish words do not start with the sp sound. In addition, it just so happens that the most common words that begin with "sp" in English begin with "esp" in Spanish. This is due to the fact that English got a lot of these words via Old French and the initial "e" from the French words was typically dropped. Therefore the "esp" Spanish words usually are the original spelling of the words, such as the name of the language itself:

español = Spanish

It is not that Spanish speakers do not have the *physical* ability to pronounce words beginning with sp in English but rather when learning another language, their pronunciation is often colored by their native tongue, hence words pronounced like this:

- Sprite - "Esprite"
- sport - "esport"
- spot - espot
- spray - espray
- sprint- esprint

So next time you hear a native Spanish speaker order an "Esprite" instead of a Sprite, you will know why!

FOOD for ⚡ Thought

Think about this....prior to picking up this book (and perhaps even as you are reading this), you spend 24 hours a day speaking your native language. A language that you know subconsciously, *unconsciously, backward and forward.* My point? **You need to dedicate *at least* 30 to 60 minutes a day to learning a language you want to learn (or at least achieve a general conversational level in)!** Stop speaking your native language for at least 30 minutes a day and dedicate it to learning Spanish! *In the scheme of a 24 hour day, 30 to 60 minutes is not that much time!*

Capítulo diecisiete (Chapter 17)

Por & Para

"FOR" + OTHER MEANINGS

Okay, I must warn you, this chapter is going to seem really confusing (*as if other previous ones have not been for you*). However, I am going to ask that you really try and wrap your mind around what I am going to say. Let's start with this.... ***Can you fathom that there would be more than one way to interpret the English word "for"***? Well, there are in Spanish! Again, let me remind you that in my opinion, Spanish is complex. For me it appears to be more complex than English, due to the myriad of grammar rules and additions that English just doesn't have. In English we have the word "for". That's the one word we have to express *For* you, For me, I am here *for* you, I am voting *for* you, etc.

In Spanish, you have two words that encompass the meaning of the English **"for"** They are:

Por & Para

However, unlike English, they take on many meanings depending on the situation and circumstances in which you are referring to. It took me months and many Spanish classes in high school and college to wrap my mind around this and to get it correct when speaking in a conversation. My goal here is to make it much simpler for you. The definitions might escape logic so not to worry, just try and think outside the box. Let's start!

Try and equate this to the lesson on masculine and feminine associations to words. To us gringos it doesn't make sense but in Spanish, it is what it is: everything takes on a gender designation. Same thinking (in theory) with por & para. Each word will have an association that is assigned to it. You just have to:

✓ **Memorize it**
✓ **Try and correlate it in the sense of what you are talking about**
✓ **Think about what purpose it will be serving.**

Here are the general uses of the words **por**:

Por (Pronounced "POOR")

- **To express movement along, through, by or around**

  Entré *por* la puerta. I entered ***through*** the door.

- **To indicate an exchange**

  Le daré veinte dólares *por* su coche. I will give you twenty dollars *in exchange for* your car.

- **To indicate time when something occurs**

  Tomamos café *por* la mañana. We have coffee *in* the morning.

- **To express means of communication or transportation**

  Comunicamos *por* telefono. We communicate *by means of* phone.

- **To express cause or reason of an action**

  Ella engordo *por falta* de ir al gimnasio. She got fat *by lack of* going to the gym.

- **Expressions (Expresiones)**

  por favor - please
  por ejemplo - for example
  por supuesto - of course
  por primera vez - for the first time
  por otra parte - on the other hand
  por fin - finally
  por lo menos - at least
  por ningún lado - nowhere
  por cierto - by the way
  por lo general - generally
  por ciento - percent
  ¿por qué? - why?
  por si acaso - just in case
  por lo menos - at least

These are very common expressions that you will come to use without even having to think about them!

Whenever you want to say "**thank you for something**" you always need to use:

Gracias por (<u>NOT</u> Gracias para)

Ejemplo: Gracias por venir - **Thank you for** coming
Gracias por el regalo - **Thank you for** the gift

Here are the general uses of the word **para:**

Para (Pronounced "PA-RAH")

- *For the purpose* of or *in order to*

  Ella vive *para* comer. She lives *in order to* eat.

  El trabaja *para* viajar. He works *in order to* travel.

- **When referring to *a specific place* that you are going to or *in the direction of***

  Voy *para* Italia. I am heading *to* Italy.

- **When referring to *a specific time* in regards to a *time frame*.**

  Necesito comprar algo *para* el lunes. I need to buy something *for* Tuesday.

  Vamos a la playa *para* el fin de semana. We are going to the beach *for* the weekend.

- **Expressions using Para**

  ¿Para qué? - For what?
  para entonces - by that time
  ser tal para cual - to be two of a kind
  para variar - for a change

The good news is that once you become familiar with the language and start listening to people speaking Spanish (*you should already be listening to a Spanish TV station or radio station at least 20-30 minutes a day per my earlier suggestion*), you will start hearing these two words used frequently in many conversations!

Okay so confused enough yet? Let me try to put it in terms of English. When trying to learn a language, in this case Spanish, we take for granted the language we already know. Por ejemplo, in English we have the words *in and inside*. Try and relate the following sentences in English to por & para.

- I am inside the house
- I am in the house

Is there really a difference between being *inside* the house or *in* the house? Inside and In the house are essentially the exact same thing, it is just another way to say it! Okay, see where I am going with this? If you were learning English for the first time, would you understand why you would say In the house vs. Inside the house when they virtually mean the same thing? Kind of mystifying, right? Well to us gringos, we don't even question it. We just say it. Same concept in Spanish and with por & para.

Another mystifying English example to help you to relate por vs. para is:

- under control
- in control

Think about these two phrases. They are virtually the same thing! Even the use of under control is a bit deceiving because under control is not literal, it is figurative! If you were learning English, would this make sense to you? Probably not, so the same thing goes for you learning Spanish. You have to wrap your mind around the meanings and concepts and do not take these comparisons at face value.

Spanish words that will confuse you at some point

la alfombra – carpet, rug
la almohada – the pillow

Capítulo dieciocho (Chapter 18)

Ser vs. Estar "<u>To Be</u> *or Not* <u>To Be</u> *That Is The Question"*

Ah yes….. That is the question! Thank you Shakespeare for your inspiring words. *Who knew that centuries later we would need Shakespeare to reference learning Spanish!*

You are going to have to really put on *your thinking caps for this lesson, as this is serious stuff.* This is one of the most important lessons to forming the foundation of a basic sentence. The state of being is a serious matter so learning how and when to use the two words that mean "to be" is very important. As you can see from the title of the chapter, there are two words in the Spanish language that mean to be. They are **ser** and **estar**. Whole books have been written about these two very important Spanish action words because they are very essential and used very often in Spanish. Why two different words you are wondering? Well, like many other lessons we have already tackled, this is just the way it is and you have to learn it.

Ser and Estar

First let's start with the **"Living in the Present tense"** of both action words (aka verbs). You will learn about action words later but it is a good idea that, when getting use these words, you keep in mind the following ways of forming them. This way you will get use to seeing them.

"The Who"	Ser	Estar
yo (I)	**soy** (I am)	**estoy** (I am)
tú (you)	**eres** (you are)	**estás** (you are)

él, ella, usted (he, she, you)	**es** (he, she, you) is	**está** (he, she, you) is
nosotros (we)	**somos** (we are)	**estamos** (we are)
ellos, ellas, ustedes (they, you all)	**son** (they, you all) are	**están** (they, you all) are

Pronunciación (Pronunciation)

Ser

Estar

soy (Pronounced like the sauce)   estoy (Pronounced S-STOY)

eres (Pronounced AIR-ACE)   estás (Pronounced S-TAHS)

es (Pronounced ACE)   está (Pronounced S-TA)

somos (Pronounced SO-MOHS)   estamos (S-TAMOS)

son (Pronounced SOWN)   están (S-TAHN)

Ser (Pronounced SEAR, as in you are going to sear a steak).... (*I'd like mine with sautéed mushrooms please*)

Think of ser as a permanent situation in regards "to being." Okay, stop right here and repeat, ***think of ser as a permanent situation in regards "to being."*** What do I mean by this? When learning the difference between ser and estar, it is going to be very helpful for you to think of using ser for **INHERENT PERMANENT** qualities and characteristics and estar as a **TEMPORARY and VARIABLE** condition.

Ser is used to express ***what*** something is, while *estar* expresses ***where*** or ***how*** it is. In general, **ser** is used to describe a person, place or thing (possession, origin, affiliation, characteristic, size, color, personality, profession). This description is something that does not change at all in some cases, or the change is gradual and slow.

109

Estar is used for location of things or people, moods, temporary feelings & physical conditions.

NON CHANGING & PERMANENT = SER
TEMPORARY & CONDITIONAL = ESTAR

The Fruit Comparisons:

One of the most useful ejemplos of expressing this difference is with an apple. In terms of the apple comparison, we are going to use green apples. When an apple is not "ripe" the color is green. Because it is not ripe yet, it is a TEMPORARY trait (because it will eventually become ripe). Due to the fact that this is a temporary trait, you would use the verb **estar** to describe it.

When a green apple becomes ripe, the color is green as well. The state of it being ripe is different than that of its permanent color, because the apple is always this color. That is a PERMANENT TRAIT and you would use the action word **ser** to describe it.

Ser	Estar
The **PERMANENT** color of an apple	**TEMPORARY** state of being unripe
La manzana es verde	La manzana está verde
(The apple is green)	(the apple is green....green meaning unripe)

NOTE how the word *"verde"* **actually changes meaning**, *depending upon whether it is used with* **ser or estar.**

Now with that being said, both ser and estar have usages that you will need to learn. Hopefully from this ejemplo, you will be able to determine when something is temporary or permanent. You have to learn the usages for both ser and estar. It is essential in order to be able to speak properly.

The following is a way to remember the uses of ser. In case each one doesn't become innately ingrained in your mind, remember the word:

| **PONCE** |

Ser:

- **Possession**: Keeping with the same theme of "state of being" is possession. This makes sense because if something belongs to someone then it is theirs. This is a permanent situation.

  Ejemplo: Este **es** mi libro. This **is** my book.

- **Occupations**: The same holds true for occupations (I know you might be thinking that people change occupations and that they can be temporary) but occupations are considered a permanent trait because you encompass what occupation you are and would always be that occupation if you never changed.

  Ejemplo:

  Soy doctor. I am a doctor.
  Soy ingeniero. I am an engineer.
  Soy abogado. I am a lawyer.
  Soy camarera. I am a waitress.

- **Nationality:** You will always be the nationality you were born with, as this a permanent state of being. You will have always have come from where you came. Therefore, use ser.

  Ejemplo: Soy americano/a. I am American.

  Soy italiano/a. I am Italian.
  Soy argentino/a. I am Argentinean.
  Soy cubano/a. I am Cuban.
  Ellos *son* de **España.** They are from Spain.

- **Characteristics**: In English when we say I'm blonde, brunette, etc. that is a permanent trait, right? (Even if after birth you have changed your hair color). If you were born a blonde, brunette, etc., you use *ser* as that is what you are. You also you ser for other characteristics, such as height, weight, size, etc.

Ejemplo:

Él *es* rubio. He is blonde.
Ella *es* delgada. She is thin.
Ellas *son* altas. The girls are tall.

- **Expressions**: The next important use of ser, (that over time you will come to use as second nature), are Impersonal Expressions. I use these expressions all of the time. They will become such a routine and a necessary part of your Spanish speaking. The only thing you have to do in the beginning is LEARN THEM. The Gringa Way is to think of the English way to say **"It is."** In English we say "It is" for a lot of things, agree? It is hot. It is raining. It is cool. It is boring. etc. In Spanish, you just use the word *es* (**él, ella, usted** form of the action word **ser) plus** whatever word you are referring to.

Ejemplos:

It is possible - **Es** posible (ACE/POE-SEE-BLAY)
It is necessary- **Es** necesario (ACE/NES-A-SAR-E-O)
It is important - **Es** importante (ACE/IM-POOR-TAHN-TAY)

P (Possession) + O (Occupations) + N (Nationality)
+ C (Characteristics) + E (Expressions) = PONCE

Create your personal story and you use it to practice. Just replace the information below with your information!

Soy de americana. **I am** from America.
Soy de Maryland. **I am** from Maryland.
Soy autora. **I am** an author.
Soy rubia. **I am** blonde.

Soy alta. **I am** tall.
Es importante aprender español. **It is** important to learn Spanish.

Now let's look at the uses for **estar**. A shortcut to remembering estar is by remembering the word:

> ### PLACE

Estar (Pronounced A-STAR, *as in you will be a star once you learn Spanish***)**

> **"to be situated"**
> If you can fit **"to be situated"** into a sentence, you would use *estar*!

- **Present** "ing" form

    Ejemplos:

    Está cantando. **He is singing.**

    Estaba estudiando en la biblioteca. **She was studying** in the library.

    Estaré trabajando el viernes. **I will be working** on Friday.

- **Location:** used to express geographic or physical locations.

    Ejemplos:

    ¿Dónde estás? Where are you?

    Estoy en la oficina. **I am in** the office.

- **Action:**

    Ejemplo: Mi hermana **está haciendo** su tarea ahora. My sister **is doing** her homework right now.

- **Condition:** To express a *temporary* condition of "how" something is

    Ejemplos:

    Estoy bien, gracias. **I am well**, thank you.

    ¿Cómo está la sopa? **How is** the soup?

    La sopa **está fría**. The soup **is cold**.

    ¿Juan **está listo** para ir? **Is Juan ready** to go?

- **Emotion:**

    Ejemplos:

    Estoy muy **nerviosa. I am** very **nervious.**

    Estás cansdada. You are tired.

    Está feliz. He is happy.

    Estamos aburridos. We are bored.

    Están emocionodos.They are excited.

<u>P</u>lace <u>L</u>ocation <u>A</u>ction <u>C</u>ondition <u>E</u>motion = PLACE

> **Can also be used when it comes before the word "de" to form various expressions**
> **Ejemplo:** Estamos **de** viaje. We are on a trip.

For how you feel or where you are, always use the verb ESTAR

Create your personal story and you use it to practice. Just replace the information below with your information!

> **Estoy en** el restaurante. **I am in** the restaurant.
> **Estoy de** viaje. **I am on** a trip.
> **Estoy en punto de** ir de compras. **I am about to go** shopping.
> **Estoy feliz** que la sopa esta caliente. **I am happy** that the soup is hot.

If you are still having trouble wrapping your mind around the difference between **ser** (permanent) and **estar** (temporary), the following ejemplos might help to shed some more light for you.

Think about the weather. The weather changes each and every day, right? Can you imagine if it snowed or rained every day? Because the weather changes every day, it is a TEMPORARY condition and therefore you use ESTAR to express weather conditions. Look at the following ejemplos:

SER (PERMANENT) ESTAR (TEMPORARY)

The sky is blue - **El cielo es azul**	It's cloudy - **Está nublado**
	It's raining - **Está lloviendo**
	It's snowing - **Está nevando**

Helpful Tips	Think about a women being pregnant. A women is not always pregnant, she is only pregnant for nine months. Being pregnant is a temporary condition; therefor you would use **estar**! (estar embarasada - to be pregnant)

These two action words are introduced to you now (before introducing other ones), because in my opinion, these are **two of the most important fundamental ones in the language.** I can promise you that you will use ser and estar in so many sentences, if not the majority of them! PLEASE learn them backwards and forwards! Even if you only master these two (IN ALL OF THEIR FORMS), you will be able to say quite a few things!

FACT:

Both of these mean **"It is good"** and they are **always** used as:

Es bueno and **Está bien**

You **CANNOT** say Está bueno or Es bien

Capítulo diecinueve (Chapter 19)

Describe it!

Try and think about the words you use throughout a day to describe someone or something. You probably don't realize it but you probably use a lot of descriptive words! You also might not realize that when you have said that *something is beautiful or that you are hot* or *that someone is jealou*s that you are being descriptive. The grammatical term for these words is adjectives. The grammatical definition (in case you are interested) is: A word that serves to modify a noun or pronoun by **describing** and **identifying** its specific **characteristics.** The word adjective itself is not important in the scheme of communication. What is important is that you know how important descriptive words are for communication. Imagine if you couldn't express how you were feeling, or how someone looked, etc. *Communication would be pretty boring, right?*

If you have ever seen the American Musical **West Side Story**, then you might recognize this song. This song is a great ejemplo of descriptive words. (http://en.wikipedia.org/wiki/West_Side_Story)

I feel <u>pretty</u>
Oh so <u>pretty</u>
I feel <u>pretty</u> and <u>witty</u> and <u>bright,</u>
And I pitty any girl who isn't me tonight.

I feel <u>charming</u>
Oh so charming
It's alarming how <u>charming</u> I feel
And so pretty that I hardly can believe I'm real.

See the pretty girl in that mirror there
Who can that <u>attractive</u> girl be?

As easy as that all sounds, there are some differences in how descriptive words are used in Spanish. *Unlike English*, where the descriptive word comes before the word it is describing (the pretty girl) in *Spanish,* **it comes *after!*** (most of the time).

English (descriptive word + *word it is describing*)	Spanish (*word it is describing* + descriptive word)
the *white* shirt	la camisa **blanca**
the **young** girl	la niña *joven*
the *delicious* dinner	la cena *deliciosa*
the *tall* boy	el muchacho ***alto***

In español, **most descriptive words change ending depending upon whether the word they modify is masculine or feminine:**

el chico **alto** - the **tall** boy
la chica **alta** - the **tall** girl
el libro **morado** - the **purple** book
la pluma **roja** - the **red** pen

Descriptive words change form depending on whether the word they describe is one or more than one things

el chico **alto**/los chicos **altos** - the **tall** boy/the **tall** boys
la chica **alta**/las chicas **altas** - the **tall** girl/the **tall** girls
el libro **rojo**/los libros **rojos** - the **red** book/the **red** books

Descriptive words that end in –*e* change form to (more than one) by adding –*s:*

La chica inteligente / **Las** chicas intelegentes

However, **descriptive words that end in –e** *do not change* **form** when *masculine* or *feminine:*

La chica **inteligente** / **El** chico **inteligente**

¡Revisemos! Let's Review!

Here are three facts that if you learn and are aware of, will help you breeze through using descriptive words in Spanish:

✓ Descriptive words that end in -o have four forms: **alto, alta, altos, altas**
✓ Descriptive words that end in **–e do not change** form regardless of gender and they have two forms: **inteligente, intelegentes**
✓ Most descriptive words that end in a *letter, not a vowel,* have two forms: **popular, populares** (you form a plural by adding **–es**)

Descriptive words that change meaning depending on placement

Some descriptive words change meaning depending on whether they come before or after the word they modify. When placed after, the descriptive word carries an objective, descriptive meaning. When placed before, the descriptive word carries a more subjective, opinionated meaning.

Ejemplos:

word being described + descriptive word	descriptive word + word being described
un *amigo* **viejo** (an old friend *meaning* an elderly friend)	un **viejo** *amigo* (an old friend *meaning* a longtime friend)
la mujer **pobre** (the poor woman *meaning* the woman without money)	la **pobre** mujer (the poor woman *meaning* the suffering woman)
un hombre **grande** (a large man)	un **gran** *hombre* (a great man, a wonderful man)

| una **gran** casa (a great house) | una casa **grande** (a big house) |

| **er & more = más** |

In English, to create a comparison, we generally "-er" (cooler, happier, stronger) or add the word "**more**" before (more intelligent, more studious, more affectionate).

| **There is no Spanish equivalent for the suffix "-er"** |

In Spanish you put the word **más (more)** in front of the descriptive word:

- **más** fuerte (stronger)
- **más** inteligente (more intelligent)
- **más** cariñoso/a (more affectionate)
- **más** atento/a (more attentive)

To indicate **"less"** rather than "more", you put the word *menos* in front of the descriptive word

- **menos** fuerte (less strong)
- **menos** inteligente (less intelligent)
- **menos** cariñoso/a (less affectionate)
- **menos** atento/a (less attentive)

The following is a list of commonly **used descriptive words**:

pequeño/a (PAY-CANE-YO/YUH)	**small**
grande (GRAHN-DAY)	**large**
joven (HO-VEN)	**young**
mayor (MY-YOUR)	**elderly**
bueno (BUAY-NO)	**good**
correcto/a (CORE-EK-TOE/A)	**right/correct**

frío /a (FREE-O/UH)	cold
equivocado/a (EK-E-VO-KAH-DOE/DUH)	wrong, incorrect
caliente (CAL-E-N-TAY)	hot, warm
calido/a (CAL-E-DOE/DUH)	warm (weather, person)
tibio(a) (TEE-B-DOE/DUH)	lukewarm
bonito/a (BOW-KNEE-TOE/TUH)	pretty
feo/a (FAY-O/UH)	ugly
largo/a (LAR-GOE/GUH)	long
corto/a (CORE-TOE/TUH)	short
fuerte (FUARE-TAY)	strong
débil (DAY-BEEL)	weak
claro/a (KLA-ROW/RUH)	light (in color) bright, clear
pasado/a (PAH-SAH-DOE/DUH)	last, previous
cercano/a (SEAR-KAHN-O/UH)	nearby
lejano/a (LAY-HAHN-O/UH)	far away

NOTE - Always remember that when you see **o/a** that this is referring to **masculine** and **feminine,** indicating you have to change the ending of the word depending if it is a masculine or feminine person, place or thing that you are talking to or about!

In Spanish, there are words that are used with descriptive words to "enhance" them and make them even more descriptive.

The following words and phrases are some of them:

más (MAHS)	**more**
menos (MAY-NOSE)	**less**
muy (MOY)	**very**
completamente (COMB-PLAY-TUH-MEN-TAY)	**completely**
bastante (BAH-STAHN-TAY)	**quite, rather**

An English word that ends in **"ly"** can change to **"mente" in Spanish.**

ly = mente

This is very simple and once you change the ending, you have an instant word in Spanish!

Let's look at how this works:

- correct**ly** - correcta**mente** (Pronounced CORE-EK-TA-MEN-TAY)

- probab**ly** - probable**mente** (Pronounced PRO-BOB-LAY-MEN-TAY)

- possib**ly** - possible**mente** (Pronounced POE-SEE-BLAY-MEN-TAY)

- definite**ly** - definitiva**mente** (Pronounced DEAF-FEEN-UH-TEE-VUH-MEN-TAY)

- slow**ly** - lenta**mente** (Pronounced LEN-TUH-MEN-TAY)

- effective**ly** - efectiva**mente** (Pronounced A-FECK-TEE-VUH-MEN-TAY)

- immediate**ly** - inmediata**mente** (Pronounced IN-MAY-DEE-AHT-AH-MEN-TAY)

- perfect**ly** - perfecta**mente** (Pronounced PER-FEC-TUH-MEN-TAY)

- rapid**ly** - rapida**mente** (Pronounced WRAP-E-DUH-MEN-TAY)

- sincere**ly** - sincera**mente** (Pronounced SEEN-SEAR-AH-MEN-TAY)

- usual**ly** - usual**mente** (Pronounced EWW-SUE-ALL-MEN-TAY)

- secret**ly** - secreta**mete** (Pronounced SAY-CRAY-TUH-MEN-TAY)

There are a few (how, when, where) words in Spanish that cannot be translated with the ending "mente" so you just have to learn these and memorize them!

- **ahora** - now (¡Vengan ahora! Come now!)

- **allí** - over there (Él duerme allí. He is sleeping over there.)

- **aquí** - here (El presidente durmió aquí. The president slept here.)

- **ayer** - yesterday (Fuimos ayer. We went yesterday.)

- **bien** - well (Usted corre bien. You run well.)

- **demasiado** - too, excessively (La muchacha come demasiado rápido. The girl eats too fast.)

- **despacio** - slowly (Ellos andan despacio. They walk slowly.)

- **mal** - badly, poorly (Ella no hace nada mal. She doesn't do anything poorly.)

- **mañana** - tomorrow (Trabajaré mañana. I will work tomorrow.)

- **siempre** - always (Ella siempre estudia. She is always studying.)

- **nunca** - never (Ella nunca trabaja. She never works.)

- **mucho** - a lot (Él habla mucho. He talks a lot.)

- **poco** - a little (Estoy un poco cansada. I am a little tired.)

- **tan** - so (La vida es tan buena. Life is so good.)

- **ya** - yet, now (Él viene ya. He's coming now.)

¡CULTURA!

Quinceañera (lit. meaning *One who is fifteen*), sometimes called "Fiesta de quince años", "Fiesta de Quinceañera", "Quince años" or simply "quince", is the celebration of a girl's fifteenth birthday in parts of Latin America and elsewhere in communities of immigrants from Latin America. This birthday is celebrated differently from any other birthday, as it marks the transition from childhood to young womanhood. The celebration, however, varies significantly across countries, with celebrations in some countries taking on more religious overtones than in others.

*This is comparable to the *Sweet Sixteen* celebrations in *the United States*

Spanish pickup lines

How are you doing? ——▶ ¿Qué tal?

You have a beautiful smile ——▶ Tienes una sonrisa hermosa (inf) Tiene una sonrisa hermosa (fomal)

You are more beautiful than the stars in the sky. ——▶ Eres más linda que las estrellas en el cielo (inf)

Usted es más linda que las estrellas en el cielo (formal)

Do you come here often? ——▶ ¿Vienes aquí a menudo? (inf)

¿Viene aquí a menudo? (formal)

Hi, I'm Mr. Right. Someone said you were looking for me ——▶ Hola, soy el hombre de sus sueños (or de tus sueños). Alguien dijo que me estabas buscando.

I am single ——▶ Soy soltero (a)

I am married ——▶ Soy casado (a)

Can I buy you a drink? ⟶ ¿Puedo invitarte a una bebida? (inf)

¿Puedo invitarle a una bebida? (formal)

Would you like to dance with me? ⟶ ¿Quieres bailar conmigo? (inf)

¿Quiere bailar conmigo? (formal)

Do you come here often? ⟶ ¿Tú vienes aquí a menudo? (inf)

¿Usted viene aquí a menudo? (formal)

May I call you? ⟶ ¿Puedo llamarte (inf)

¿Puedo llamarle? (formal)

Are you free this evening? ⟶ ¿ Estas disponible esta noche? (inf)

¿ Está disponible esta noche? (formal)

Spanish words that will confuse you at some point

el cuento - the story
la cuenta - the account, the check (as in a restaurant check)

Capítulo veinte (Chapter 20)

Connect it!

Think of this section as a game of *Connect the Dots* but with using little words to connect them! As in English, in Spanish there are little words that **connect** one part of a sentence to another and indicate movement, time, position, and relationship among two or more objects within a sentence. (In grammar terms, they are called prepositions) but you just need to know what these words are and what they stand for. These words are used in every day conversation.

Spanish connecting words DO NOT take on masculine/feminine or singular/plural forms.

They will always have the same form

You have already learned two of the most important connectivity words, *por y para* so let's learn some important other ones!

español	inglés
a (AH)	at, to
ante (AHN-TAY)	before, compared to
bajo (BAH-HO)	under, below
con (CONE)	with
contra (CONE-TRA)	against
de (DAY)	of, about
desde (DES-DAY)	since, from

durante (DOOR-AHN-TAY)	during, for
en (IN)	in, on, into, by, at
entre (N-TRAY)	between, among, amongst
excepto (X-CEP-TOE)	with the exception of
hacia (AH-C-UH)	towards, about, around
hasta (AH-STA)	as far as, up to, until
mediante (MED-E-AHN-TAY)	by means of
según (SAY-GOON)	according to
sin (SEEN)	without
sobre (SO-BRAY)	on top of, over, above, about
antes de (AHN-TASE/DAY)	before
cerca de (SEAR-KA/DAY)	near, close to
debajo de (DAY-BAH-HOE/DAY)	under, underneath
delante de (DAY-LAHN-TAY/DAY)	in front of
dentro de (DEN-TROE/DAY)	in, inside, into, within
después de (DAY-SPUACE/DAY)	after
detrás de (DAY-TRAS/DAY)	behind
encima de (N-SEE-MUH/DAY)	on top of, above
enfrente de (IN-FREN-TAY/DAY)	in front of, across from
fuera de (FUER-UH/DAY)	except for, apart from
junto a (HOON-TOE/AH)	next to, right by, near
lejos de (LAY-HOSE/DAY)	far away from

There are two very important and very commonly used connectivity words in Spanish. **Don't let size fool you!** Just because these two words only contain one and two letters, they are essential and you will hear these two words used everywhere. They are:

> a & de

The connecting word **"a"** (Pronounced "AH") means **"to"** and **"at"**

The *a* (referred to as the personal a in grammar world) is really used when:

✓ You need to say **to** or **at** in a sentence:
  • Viajaron **a** Madrid. = They traveled *to* Madrid.
  • Llegaron **a** las dos. = They arrived *at* two o'clock.

✓ You are talking about or mentioning a specific person or people and they are the **main object** of the sentence:
  • I saw Teresa. = Yo vi *a* Teresa.
  • I sent the letter to Juan. = Le envié la carta *a* Juan.
  • I remember my grandfather. = Recuerdo *a* mi abuelo.

 The **only difference** between the English sentence and Spanish is the word **"a"**

"a" is also a very commonly used as a contraction *(and no I am not talking labor contractions here)*. When "a" is combined with "el" (which you already learned means **"the"**), the "e" in "el" is dropped and it becomes "al". This takes on the meaning of **"to the"**.

> a + el = **al** and means **"to the"**

Ejemplos:

• Voy *al* cine. = I go *to the* theater.

129

- Va *al* restaurant con ella. = He goes *to the* restaurant with her.
- ¡Al coche! = *To the* car!
- ¿Quieres ir conmigo *al* parque? = Do you want to go with me *to the* park?

de

| "of" "from" "of something" "of somewhere" |

The connecting word **"de"** (Pronounced "DAY") means **"of"** and **"from"**

In Spanish, *de* is also used to express where something or someone comes from or what something is made up of. In Spanish, you have to think of everything (okay maybe not everything but a lot of things) as being **"of something"** or **"of somewhere"**. In English, we say a sentence straightforward but in Spanish you have to say **"de" something/somewhere**.

Por ejemplo (For example):

- "A twelve year old boy" translates to "Un muchacho **de** doce años" in Spanish (literally translating to *a boy of twelve years)*

- "A silver ring" translates to "Un anillo *de* plata" in Spanish (literally translating to a ring *of* silver)

- "A cheeseburger" translates to "Una hamburgesa *de* queso" in Spanish (literally a hamburger *of* cheese)

- "Don Quixote *de* La Mancha" is used to indicate where Don Quixote comes from (he comes *from* la Mancha, a provence in Spain.)

's

---

de is also the equivalent to the English "'s" (aka the possessive form)

- El clima cálido **de** Sevilla = Sevilla's warm climate.
- La hermana **de** Juan = Juan's sister.
- El carro **de** mi hermana = My sister's car

"de" is very commonly used as a contraction. When "de" is combined with "el" (which means "the") the "e" in "el" is dropped and it becomes "del". This takes on the meaning of **"of the"** or **"from the"**

---

de + el = del and means "of the" or "from the"

However, *de* **does not** contract to *del* when followed by **él** ("he") or a proper person or place name, thus:

- Soy amiga **de** *él* - I am his friend.
- Es el alcalde **de** *El Escorial* - He is the mayor of El Escorial.

Okay, depending on how many times a day you pick up this book and practice. My suggestion to you at this point is to put down the book for a day, walk to a wall and bang your head against it a couple times…. no really (***Don't bang it to hard as you are going to need some brain cells for the next chapter***) but do bang it a couple of times. After you have done this, resume reading this book and let's begin with the next chapter!

Capítulo veintiuno (Chapter 21)

WARNING: Don't Catch Verbitis!

Symptoms: Extreme confusion, Lack of motivation, Headaches

Needs to be treated as soon as you contract it!

Verb: A verb is a part of speech that expresses action, existence, or occurrence

Verb conjugation - refers to the process of changing a verb form to provide information about **who** is performing the action of the verb (person) and **when** the action is taking place (tense)

This lesson, verbs (grammar term), or **action words** (as The Gringa Way refers to them), will probably be the biggest hurdle ![hurdle] in your learning of the Spanish language. *Action words are the meat and potatoes of communication and in Spanish, the most complicated to learn!* Learning action words can prove to be much more of a challenge than even learning other tough subjects such as ser & estar and por & para. Why you ask? Well, Spanish has more action word tenses than English and in addition to this, the action words are very complex. There are three different type endings, there are action words that change form when conjugated and there is a special form called the *subjunctive*, which actually requires you to have to change the ending of the action word when you have two subjects you are speaking about in one sentence. YIKES!

Here is the goods news! In this book, *Volume 1*, you are only going to be presented with the **most basic**, action word tenses. They are:

- **Living in the Present** - Belonging to the present time (**Doing it now**)

- **Been there done that** - Already happened (**Did it**)
- **Going to do it** - Something that will be done in time to come (**Will do it**)

The rest of the tenses will be presented for your learning in Volume 2. This is due to the fact that if you were to have all of the tenses thrown at you at once, you would most likely feel very overwhelmed and frustrated, making you not want to continue to learn. Learning action words can be very stressful and I do not want you to feel stressed or overwhelmed at this point. I also want you to master these three tenses before you move onto more intricate ones. **By learning these three now, you will be able to make complete sentences and communicate!**

The most basic and easiest action word form

In grammar world, this is called the **infinitive** but you don't need to worry about the word, just the format.

The infinitive is the most basic and the easiest form because it does not need to be conjugated! Yes, that is right, you can use it the exact way it is! It is also the form that appears in dictionaries. **Unlike the conjugated forms,** (the ones used most often in speech and the ones that will cause you the most frustration), **an infinitive standing alone says nothing about how many people are performing the action or when.**

In English, it is the combination of the word "to" +whatever action you are performing

(to speak, to eat, to drink, to walk)

Infinitive action words in Spanish actually contain the word "to" in them (so you only need to choose the action word you want to use).

hablar (to speak), comer (to eat), beber (to drink), andar (to walk)

One of the most common and most widely used way of the infinitive form is the combination of the **conjugated action word** ir + a + infinitive.

> **ir + a + infinitive = to be going to do something** (in the near future)

ir conjugated = I go - **voy**
you go - **vas**
he, she, it goes - **va**
we go - **vamos**
they go - **van**

Ejemplos:

- **I am going to take** my sister to her house. = **Voy a llevar** a mi hermana a su casa
- Heather **is going to talk** with her boyfriend. = Heather **va a conversar** con su novio.
- Juan **is going to read** the book. = Juan **va a leer** el libro.

> The infinitive can also take on the form of the English ending of **"ing"**

Ejemplos:

- **Caminar** es una forma saludable de ejercicio. = **Walking** is a healthy form of exercise.
- Es prohibido **fumar**. = **Smoking** is prohibited.
- Pienso **salir** contigo. = I'm thinking about **going out** with you.
- Muestre moderación en el **comer**. = Show moderation in **eating**.

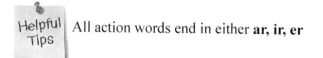 All action words end in either **ar, ir, er**

Are you felling *regular* today?

Okay so who knew words could be regular or irregular? Sounds wierd, right? Up until now, you have probably only associated regularity and irregularity with bowel movements! Believe it or not, action words have two forms, either regular or irregular. However, we are not going to focus on what is which because the most important things is for you to learn the actions words as is, not to focus (at least initially) on what is regular and what isn't.

For your knowledge:

A **regular action word** is one that follows a regular pattern in the way they are conjugated.

An **irregular action word** is one that cannot be conjugated in a regular pattern. In contrast to regular ones, *irregular* are those that fall outside the standard patterns of conjugation in the languages in which they occur.

"Living in the present" action word endings:

Person	ar	er	ir
I **(yo)**	o	o	o
you **(tú)**	as	es	es
he, she, it **(usted)**	a	e	e
we **(nosotros)**	amos	emos	imos
they, you all **(ustedes)**	an	en	en

"Been there, done that" action word endings:

Person	ar	er	ir
I **(yo)**	é	í	í
you **(tú)**	aste	iste	iste
he, she, it **(usted)**	ó	ió	ió
we **(nosotros)**	amos	imos	imos
they, you all **(ustedes)**	aron	ieron	ieron

"Going to do it sometime in the future" action word endings:

Person	ar, er, ir
I (**yo**)	(infinitive) + é
you (**tú**)	(infinitive) + ás
he, she, it (**usted**)	(infinitive) + á
we (**nosotros**)	(infinitive) + emos
they, you all (**ustedes**)	(infinitive) + án

NOTE - There are two ways to say the future tense. You just learned one (ir + a + infinitive) or the one above, the infinitive of the action word + the proper ending (ex. comeré, comerás, comerá, comeremos, comerán)

As the old adage goes, *"it is not quantity, rather quality that counts"*. This holds true when it comes to Spanish action words. There are key ones that are used very often and in most Spanish speech. The following cover the basic way to express a lot of what you will need to say. This is not to say there are not hundreds of additional valuable action words that you will need to learn, but rather it is to start off learning the most fundamental ones.

Popular Action Words

"hablar" (AH-BLAR)

"to talk"

	Present	Past	Future
I (yo)	hablo	hablé	hablaré
	(I talk)	(I talked)	(I will talk)
you (tú)	hablas	hablaste	hablarás
he, she, it, you (él, ella, usted)	habla	habló	hablará
we (nosotros)	hablamos	hablamos	hablaremos
you all, they (ustedes)	hablan	hablaron	hablarán

"com**er**" (CO-MEER)

"to eat"

	Present	Past	Future
I (yo)	como (I eat)	comí (I ate)	comeré (I will eat)
you (tú)	comes	comiste	comerás
he, she, it, you (él, ella, usted)	come	comió	comerá
we (nosotros)	comemos	comimos	comeremos
you all, they (ustedes)	comen	comieron	comerán

"viv**ir**" (V-VEER)

"to live"

	Present	Past	Future
I (yo)	vivo (I live)	viví (I lived)	viviré (I will live)
you (tú)	vives	viviste	vivirás
he, she, it, you (él, ella, usted)	vive	vivió	vivirá
we (nosotros)	vivimos	vivimos	viviremos
you all, they (ustedes)	viven	vivieron	vivirán

"s**er**" (SEAR)

(to be: permanent state of being**)**

	Present	Past	Future
I (yo)	soy (I am)	fui (I was)	seré (I will be)
you (tú)	eres	fuiste	serás
he, she, it, you (él, ella, usted)	es	fue	será
we (nosotros)	somos	fuimos	seremos
you all, they (ustedes)	son	fueron	serán

Most common expressions using ser (*conjugate action word depending on subject*):

- **Ser de** - to be from (a city, country)
- **así es la vida** - such is life (this is an expression and does not need any conjugation)
- **ser uña y carne** - to be as close as can be

"estar" (S-STAR)

(**to be**: temporary: location, to be situated)

	Present	Past	Future
I (yo)	estoy (I am)	estuve (I was)	estaré (I will be)
you (tú)	estas	estuviste	estarás
he, she, it, you (él, ella, usted)	está	estuvo	estará
we (nosotros)	estamos	estuvimos	estaremos
you all, they (ustedes)	están	estuvieron	estarán

Most common expressions using estar (*conjugate action word depending on subject*):

- **estar listo** - to be ready
- **estar + "ing"** - to be doing something
- **estar al corriente de** - to be up to date on
- **estar de acuerdo** - to be in agreement with
- **estar de buen humor** - to be in a good mood
- **estar de mal humor** - to be in a bad mood
- **estar de vacaciones** - to be on vacation
- **estar de vuelta** - to be back, to have returned
- **estar en buenas condiciones** - to be in good shape
- **estar en malas condiciones** - to be in bad shape
- **estar en las nubes** - to be in the clouds (figurative)

"ir" (EAR)

"to go"

	Present	Past	Future
I (yo)	voy (I go)	fui (I went)	iré (I will go)
you (tú)	vas	fuiste	irás
he, she, it, you (él, ella, usted)	va	fue	irá
we (nostros)	vamos	fuimos	iremos
you all, they (ustedes)	van	fueron	irán

Most common expressions using ir (*conjugate action word depending on subject*):

- **ir de compras** - to go shopping
- **ir a pie** - to walk (on foot)
- **ir en** + (carro, autobús, tren, barco) - to travel by (car, bus, train, boat)
- **ir andando** - to go walking
- **ir corriendo** - to go running
- **ir de, ir con** - to be dressed in

"hacer" (AH-SEAR)

"to do, to make"

	Present	Past	Future
I (yo)	hago (I do, I make)	hice (I made)	haré (I will do/ make)
you (tú)	haces	hiciste	harás
he, she, it, you (él, ella, usted)	hace	hizo	hará
we (nosotros)	hacemos	hicimos	haremos
you all, they (ustedes)	hacen	hicieron	harán

Most common expressions using hacer (*conjugate action word depending on subject*):

hace calor - to be hot (weather)
hace frío - to be cold (weather)
hacer una broma - to play a joke
hacer la maleta - to pack a suitcase
hacer caso de - to pay attention to
hacer un papel - to play a role
hacer una pregunta - to ask a question
hacer la vista gorda - to turn a blind eye
hacerle falta - to need
hacer un mandado - to run an errand
hagas lo que quiera (informal) - Do what you want
hace poco - a little while ago
hacer un viaje - to take a trip
hacerse - to become

"ver" (VEER)

"to see"

	Present	**Past**	**Future**
I (yo)	veo (I see)	vi (I saw)	veré (I will see)
you (tú)	ves	viste	verás
he, she, it, you (él, ella, usted)	ve	vio	verá
we (nosotros)	vemos	vimos	veremos
you all, they (ustedes)	ven	vieron	verán

"poder" (POE-DEER)

"to be able to"

	Present	Past	Future
I (yo)	puedo (I can)	pude (I could)	podré (I will be able to)
you (tú)	puedes	pudiste	podrás
he, she, it, you (él, ella, usted)	puede	pudo	podrá
we (nosotros)	podemos	pudimos	podremos
you all, they (ustedes)	pueden	pudieron	podrán

"decir" (DAY-SEAR)

"to say"

	Present	Past	Future
I (yo)	digo (I say)	dije (I said)	diré (I will say)
you (tú)	dices	dijiste	dirás
he, she, it, you (él, ella, usted)	dice	dijo	dirá
we (nosotros)	decimos	dijimos	diremos
you all, they (ustedes)	dicen	dijeron	dirá

"empezar" (M-PAY-ZAR)

"to start, to begin"

	Present	Past	Future
I (yo)	empiezo (I start)	empecé (I started)	empezaré (I will start)
you (tú)	empiezas	empezaste	empezarás
he, she, it, you (él, ella, usted)	empieza	empezó	empezará
we (nosotros)	empezamos	empezamos	empezaremos
you all, they (ustedes)	empiezan	empezaron	empezarán

"dar" (DAR)

"to give"

	Present	Past	Future
I (yo)	doy (I give)	di (I gave)	daré (I will give)
you (tú)	das	diste	darás
he, she, it, you (él, ella, usted)	da	dio	dará
we (nosotros)	damos	dimos	daremos
you all, they (ustedes)	dan	dieron	darán

comer (CO-MEAR)

"to eat"

	Present	Past	Future
I (yo)	como (I eat)	comí (I ate)	comeré (I will eat)
you (tú)	comes	comiste	comerás
he, she, it, you (él, ella, usted)	come	comió	comerá
we (nosotros)	comemos	comimos	comeremos
you all, they (ustedes)	comen	comieron	comerán

venir (VAY-NEAR)

"to come"

	Present	Past	Future
I (yo)	vengo (I come)	vine (I came)	vendré (I will come)
you (tú)	vienes	viniste	vendrás
he, she, it, you (él, ella, usted)	viene	vino	vendrá
we (nosotros)	venimos	vinimos	vendremos
you all, they (ustedes)	vienen	vinieron	vendrán

"querer" (CARE-AIR)

"to want"

	Present	Past	Future
I (yo)	quiero (I want)	quise (I wanted)	querré (I will want)
you (tú)	quieres	quisiste	querrás
he, she, it, you (él, ella, usted)	quiere	quiso	querrá
we (nosotros)	queremos	quisimos	querremos
you all, they (ustedes)	quieren	quisieron	querrán

"tener" (TAY-NEAR)

"to have"

	Present	Past	Future
I (yo)	tengo (I have)	tuve (I had)	tendré (I will have)
you (tú)	tienes	tuviste	tendrás
he, she, it, you (él, ella, usted)	tiene	tuvo	tendrá
we (nosotros)	tenemos	tuvimos	tendremos
you all, they (ustedes)	tienen	tuvieron	tendrán

NOTE In Spanish, tener is used more widely than the action word to have in English. *It's not only used to express possession* but also to help express many other idioms *of emotions and state of being.*

Ejemplos:

Tengo 20 años. I´m 20 years old.
Tengo hambre. I'm hungry.
Tengo sed. I am thirsty.
Tengo calor. I am hot. (temperature wise)

Tener que + infinitive = "To have to" + infinitive of action word

Ejemplos:

Tengo que ir al banco. = I have to go to the bank.
Tengo que ir de compras. = I have to go shopping.
Tienes que hacer tu tarea. = You have to do your homework.
Ella tiene que ir al baile. = She has to go to the dance.

Most common expressions using tener (*conjugate action word depending on subject*)**:**

tener frío - to be cold
tener sueño - to be sleepy
tener razón - to be right
no tener razón - to be wrong
tener prisa - to be in a hurry
tener cuidado - to be careful
tener suerte - to be lucky
tener miedo - to be afraid

tener ganas de + (infinitive) - to feel like doing something. **NOTE** - *you have to add in the action word that you feel like doing.* **Ejemplos:** Tengo ganas de ir de compras - I feel like going shopping. Tengo ganas de hacer un viaje - I feel like going on a trip.

haber (AH-BEAR)

"to have"

	Present	Past	Future
I (yo)	he (I have)	hube (I had)	habré (I will have)
you (tú)	has	hubiste	habrás
he, she, it, you (usted)	ha	hubo	habrá
we (nosotros)	hemos	hubimos	habremos
you all, they (ustedes)	han	hubieron	habrán

As you may have just noticed, both action words tener and haber listed above mean **"to have"**. However the meaning to have and the way they are used is unique to each action word:

Tener means to have in the sense of **possession of something** or **some (tangible item)**

- Tengo un libro en casa. = I have a book at home.
- Tengo un coche. = I have one car.

Haber is usually used much like the English "to have" (as a helper action word to convey an action):

- I have read four books this month. = **He leido** cuatro libros este mes.
- He has gone to the movies five times this year. = Él **ha ido** al cine cinco veces durante este año.

Focus on the difference between these two action words with the same meaning: *The difference is straightforward*

Tengo tres libros. **I have** three books.
He leído tres libros, **I have read** three books.

"saber" (SAH-BEAR)

"to know"

	Present	Past	Future
I (yo)	sé (I know)	supe (I knew)	sabré (I will know)
you (tú)	sabes	supiste	sabrás
he, she, it, you (él, ella, usted)	sabe	supo	sabrá
we (nosotros)	sabemos	supimos	sabremos
you all, they (ustedes)	saben	supieron	sabrán

"conocer" (CO-NO-SEAR)

"to know"

	Present	Past	Future
I (yo)	conozco (I know)	conocí (I knew)	conoceré (I will know)
you (tú)	conoces	conociste	conocerás
he, she, it, you (él, ella, usted)	conoce	conoció	conocerá
we (nosotros)	conocemos	conocimos	conoceremos
you all, they (ustedes)	conocen	conocieron	conocerán

As you may have just noticed, both these action words, *saber* and *conocer* listed above mean **"to know"**. Yes, that's right, more words with the same meaning! However, the meaning of them and the way they are used is unique to each action word:

Conocer *comes from the same root as the English word "cognition" and* means "to know someone" or "meeting someone for the first time, as well as "to be familiar with."

Saber *on the other hand, means* **"to know a fact," "to know how"** or **"to possess knowledge"** and it used generally speaking *about knowing something*, **NOT** *someone!*

NOTE

You **CANNOT** ever say "Yo *sé* a alguien" (I know someone)
ALWAYS have to use "Yo *conozco* a alguien"

Ejemplos usando conocer. Examples using conocer. (*conjugate action words depending on subject*).

* I met my teacher yesterday for the first time. = **Conocí** a mi profesor ayer por primera vez.
* I know a lot of people. = **Conozco** a mucha gente.
* Do you know her brother? = ¿**Conoce** a su hermano?
* I met my wife in Spain. = **Conocí** a mi esposa en España.

Ejemplos usando saber. Examples using saber:

* I don't know anything. = No sé nada.
* I do not know how to play football. = No sé cómo jugar el futbol.
* I don't know the answer. = No sé la respuesta.

The two action words are also used in a number of phrases. The following ones listed are among the most common. (*conjugate action words depending on subject*):

* **a saber** - namely
* **conocer al dedillo** o **conocer palmo a palmo** - to know like the palm of one's hand
* **conocer de vista** - to know by sight
* **cuando lo supe** - when I found out
* **dar a conocer** - to make known
* **darse a conocer** - to make oneself known
* **no saber ni jota de algo** - to not have a clue about something
* **no se sabe** - It is not known
* **para que lo sepas** - for your information
* **que yo sepa** - as far as I know

- **¿Quién sabe?** - Who knows?
- **se sabe que** - it is known that
- **¡Yo que sé!** - How am I supposed to know!

"leer" (LAY-AIR)

"to read"

	Present	Past	Future
I (yo)	leo (I read)	leí (I read)	leeré (I will read)
you (tú)	lees	leíste	leerás
he, she, it, you (él, ella, usted)	lee	leyó	leerá
we (nosotros)	leemos	leímos	leeremos
you all, they (ustedes)	leen	leyeron	leerán

"jugar" (WHO-GAR)

"to play"

	Present	Past	Future
I (yo)	juego (I play)	jugué (I played)	jugaré (I will play)
you (tú)	juegas	jugaste	jugarás
he, she, it, you (él, ella, usted)	juega	jugó	jugará
we (nosotros)	jugamos	jugamos	jugaremos
you all, they (ustedes)	juegan	jugaron	jugarán

"salir" (SAH-LEER)

"to leave, to go out with"

	Present	Past	Future
I (yo)	salgo (I leave)	salí (I left)	saldré (I will leave)
you (tú)	sales	saliste	saldrás
he, she, it, you (él, ella, usted)	sale	salió	saldrá
we (nosotros)	salimos	salimos	saldremos
you all, they (ustedes)	salen	salieron	saldrán

"poner" (POE-NEAR)

"to put"

	Present	Past	Future
I (yo)	pongo (I put)	puse (I put)	pondré (I will put)
you (tú)	pones	pusiste	pondrás
he, she, you (él, ella, usted)	pone	puso	pondrá
we (nosotros)	ponemos	pusimos	pondremos
you all, they (ustedes)	ponen	pusieron	pondrán

"dormir" (DOOR-MEER)

"to sleep"

	Present	Past	Future
I (yo)	duermo (I sleep)	dormí (I slept)	dormiré (I will sleep)
you (tú)	duermes	dormiste	dormirás
he, she, you (él, ella, usted)	duerme	durmió	dormirá
we (nosotros)	dormimos	dormimos	dormiremos
you all, they (ustedes)	duermen	durmieron	dormirán

"pedir" (PAY-DEER)

"to ask/to request"

	Present	Past	Future
I (yo)	pido (I ask)	pedí (I asked)	pediré (I will ask)
you (tú)	pides	pediste	pedirás
he, she, you (él, ella, usted)	pide	pidió	pedirá
we (nosotros)	pedimos	pedimos	pediremos
you all, they (ustedes)	piden	pidieron	pedirán

"preguntar" (PREY-GOON-TAR)

"to ask"

	Present	Past	Future
I (yo)	pregunto (I ask)	pregunté (I asked)	preguntaré (I will ask)
you (tú)	preguntas	preguntaste	preguntarás
he, she, you (él, ella, usted)	pregunta	preguntó	preguntará
we (nosotros)	preguntamos	preguntamos	preguntaremos
you all, they (ustedes)	preguntan	preguntaron	preguntarán

Pedir vs. Preguntar

As you may have just noticed, both these verbs, **pedir** y **preguntar** listed above mean **"to ask"**. However, the meaning and the way they are used, is unique to each:

pedir - to ask for, to request a service or favor (**think of pedir as a solicitation for something**)

• Ella ya le **pidió** el dinero. She already asked him for the money.

preguntar - ask a question, or request information

• Siempre me **preguntas** lo mismo. You're always asking me the same question.

"traer" (TRA-EAR)

"to bring"

	Present	Past	Future
I (yo)	traigo (I bring)	traje (I brought)	traeré (I will bring)
you (tú)	traes	trajiste	traerás
he, she, it, you (él, ella, usted)	trae	trajo	traerá
we (nosotros)	traemos	trajimos	traeremos
you all, they (ustedes)	traen	trajeron	traerán

"pensar"

"to think"

	Present	Past	Future
I (yo)	pienso (I think)	pensé (I thought)	pensaré (I will think)
you (tú)	piensas	pensaste	pensarás
he, she, it, you (él, ella, usted)	piensa	pensó	pensará
we (nosotros)	pensamos	pensamos	pensaremos
you all, they (ustedes)	piensan	pensaron	pensarán

"volver" (VOL-VEER)

"to come back, to return"

	Present	Past	Future
I (yo)	vuelvo (I return)	volví (I returned)	volveré (I will return)
you (tú)	vuelves	volviste	volverás
he, she, it, you (él, ella, usted)	vuelve	volvió	volverá
we (nosotros)	volvemos	volvimos	volveremos
you all, they (ustedes)	vuelven	volvieron	volverán

What are you **"ing"**?

In other words, **what are you doing?** The **"ing"** form in English is the easiest form to remember and use in Spanish.

---

ing = **ando** (add this to the end of **-ar verbs**)

ing = **iendo** (and add this to the end of **-er, -ir** verbs)

yendo if the stem ends in a vowel (leer = leer - er + yendo = leyendo)

Ejemplos:

hab<u>**ar**</u> = hab<u>**ando**</u> (you just drop the –ar and add –ando) = talking

com<u>**er**</u> = com<u>**iendo**</u> (you just drop the –er and add –iendo) = eating

viv<u>**ir**</u> = viv<u>**iendo**</u> (you just drop the –ir and add – iendo) = living

I am sure you are wondering how you say that you yourself are "ing" or someone else is "ing". It is a really easy formula.....you just have to use the action word estar!

Estar + **"ando" "iendo"** form of action word = **to be doing something**

You have already learned the conjugations for **estar** so here are ejemplos with the **"ing"** format:

- **Estoy traba<u>jando</u>** - I am **working**

  (from traba<u>**jar**</u> = to work)

- **Estas jug<u>ando</u>** - You are **playing**

  (from juag<u>**ar**</u> = to play)

- **Esta vol<u>viendo</u>** - He, she or you are **returning**

(from volv**er** = to return)

- **Estamos imprimiendo** - We are printing

  (from imprim**ir** = to print)

- **Estan le<u>y</u>endo** - They are reading

  (from le**er** = to read)

The ando/iendo form is also used with the action word **ir** *to express an action which is gradual*:

La economía china **<u>va</u> mejor<u>ando</u>**. (Chinese economy **is getting better**.)

You will hear people a lot of times adding "**ado**" and "**ido**" to the end of action words. When they add these two endings, it usually indicates that the action has been complete.

Ejemplos:

Hablar (to speak) ⟶ hablado (spoken) He **habl<u>ado</u>** con ella. **I have spoken** to her.

Comer (to eat) ⟶ comido (eaten) Ya han **com<u>ido</u>**. They **have** already **eaten.**

Entender (to understand) ⟶ **Entend<u>ido</u>**? Understood?

<u>RECAP</u>

-ar verbs

Root	Ending	Tranlsation
Trabaj-	ar	To work
Trabaj-	o	I work
Trabaj-	é	I worked
Trabaj-	aré	I will work

-er verbs

Root	Ending	Translation
Com-	er	To eat
Com-	o	I eat
Com-	í	I ate
Com-	eré	I will eat

-ir verbs

Root	Ending	Translation
Viv-	ir	To live
Viv-	o	I live
Viv	í	I lived
Viv-	iré	I will live

Spanish words that will confuse you at some point

el puerto – the port
la puerta – the door

CAPÍTULO VEINTIDÓS (CHAPTER 22)

You don't se!

"You did it to yourself"

In Spanish, if you want to say that you do something to yourself or someone does something to themselves, all you have to do is tack on **"se"** to the end of an action word.

Ejemplos:

lavar = to wash *but* **lavar*se*** means "to wash oneself"

levantar = to raise up *but* **levantar*se*** means to "raise oneself up"

sentar = to sit *but* **sentar*se*** means to "sit oneself down"

sentir = to feel but **sentir*se*** means to "how you as a person feels"

Use **me** to say "I am doing it **to myself**", use **te** to say you are doing it **"to yourself"**, use **se** to say they are doing it to **"his, her or themselves"**, use **nos** to say **"we are doing it to ourselves"**.

Ejemplos: Lavarse

me lavo = **I** wash myself

te lavas = **you** wash yourself

se lava = **he, she, you** washes themselves

nos lavamos = **we** wash ourselves

se lavan = **they** wash themselves

Ejemplos: Sentirse

Me siento avergonzada. = **I feel** embarrassed.

¿Te sientes avergonzado? = **Do you feel** embarrased?

¿Se siente avergonzado? = **Does he/she feel** embarrased? Do you (formal) feel embarrased?

Nos sentimos avergonzados. = **We feel** embarrased.

Se sienten avergonzadas. = **They feel** embarrased.

How to be impersonal

Impersonal expressions are used when the subject of a action word is **unspecified** or **unknown** (but is human). They are mostly used to make general statements. In Spanish, it is really easy to form a sentence like this. (It is called the impersonal and passive *se* in the Spanish grammar world because there is no specified subject). You just have to add **se** in front of a third person singular or plural action word (*whatever action word you need to express your action*) and voila, that makes it **impersonal!**

- **Se dice que es bueno para comer.** - It is said that it is good to eat.
- **Se escribe** el libro en ingles. - The book is written in English.
- **Se habla** español en Mexico. - Spanish is spoken in Mexico.

Another use of this form is asking how to spell a word or what a word means. You will use this format a lot when you are speaking Spanish and you need to know how to say something and have to ask how to say it.

- ¿Cómo **se escribe** chocolate? **How do you spell** chocolate?
- ¿Cómo **se dice** book en español? **How do you say** book in Spanish?
- ¿Cómo **se llama** la pelicula que viste anoche?" **What is the name** of the movie you saw last night?

NOTE The difference between the Spanish and English translation is that the English translation contains "one," "they," or "you," but there is no subject specified in Spanish (which is what makes it impersonal).

---

llevar + period of time = It has been + period of time

I have been singing for 5 years = ***Llevo cinco años*** cantando
We have been studying for four years = ***Llevamos cuatro años*** estudiando
They have been traveling for two years = ***Llevan dos años*** viajando

---

CAPÍTULO VEINTITRÉS (CHAPTER 23)

Commands (Mandatos)

Nobody likes to be told what do, right? Who likes commands? Well as much as we might not like commands, they are necessary for communication purposes.

Spanish commands are just that, commands. They are used the same way they are in English, to directly address someone and give them an order. Commands in Spanish are probably some of the easiest words to put together, *after you have learned* ar, er, ir *action words.*

Hopefully you remember from the earlier chapters that there are informal (tú/you) and formal (usted/you) ways of speaking to people in Spanish. (In English there are as well. However, the difference is that in English, the action words endings are the same regardless. **It is simply the salutation that varies....for ejemplo (Sir, Maam, Miss, Mrs.).**

The main three factors you have to keep in mind when giving a command in Spanish are the following:

✓ Are you speaking to someone informal or formal?
✓ Are you speaking to one person (singular) or more than one person (plural)?
✓ Are you telling someone (to do something) or (not don't do something)?

Telling people you know, such as friends, family, children, coworkers **to do something (tú/you) commands**

This form of a "**tú**" (you) command is fairly easy to learn, in that it is almost always identical to the él, ella, usted form of Spanish action words **Living in the present tense.** Why are these commands easy to learn you ask? The present form is the simplest form. *As long as you know the present tense; you also know how to give a command!*

Here is how it works. All you have to do is basically drop the "-r" off the infinitive of the action word and voila! *A command is born*! I know, it sounds too easy to be true....but it really is this easy!

(hablar (-r) = *habla*)

Action word ending	Infinitive	Command	Ejemplo
-ar	hablar (to talk)	Habla	**Habla** conmigo. (**Talk** with me.)

(comer (-r) = *come*)

Action word ending	Infinitive	Command	Ejemplo
-er	comer (to eat)	Come	**Come** la cena. (**Eat** dinner.)

(escribir (-ir) (+ e) = *escribe*)

Action word ending	Infinitive	Command	Ejemplo
-ir	escribir (to write)	Escribe	**Escribe** la carta. (**Write** the letter.)

*Notice that the *ir* action word endings are the only exception where the ending changes from "ir" to an "e"

Simplified! If you have an "ar" and "er" ending action word, you just have to drop the *r* and you have a command! With "ir" verb ending, you just simply drop the "ir" and replace it with *e.*

The "informal" commands use the (él, ella, usted) form of action words

Ejemplos:

<u>**Comprar**</u> (to buy)

Compr<u>a</u> (tú) el anillo - (You) buy the ring

<u>**Beber**</u> (to drink)

Beb<u>e</u> (tú) la leche - (You) drink the milk

<u>**Exigir**</u> (to demand)

Exig<u>e</u> (tú) la respuesta - (You) demand the answer

NOTE The below action words are the "not normal form" commands, which means that they do not follow the same "rules" as above.

You have learned these action words in their (present, past and future) forms in the previous chapter, so the action words should not look as foreign to you at this point. There are only nine "not normal" action words when giving informal commands. You just have to memorize the following ones, as there really is no rhyme or reason as to why they are done differently.

Put on your memorization caps!

Action word	You (tú) command	Ejemplo
decir (to say, to tell)	**di**	Dime la verdad (Tell me the truth)
hacer (to do, to make)	**haz**	Hazlo (Do it)
ir (to go)	**ve**	Ve (Go)
irse (to go away)	**vete**	Vete (Go away)

poner (to put, to place)	pon	Ponlo en mi habitación (Put it in my room)
salir (to go out, to leave)	sal	Sal de aquí (Get out of here)
ser (to be)	sé	Sé bueno (Be good)
tener (to have)	ten	Ten cuidado (Be careful)
venir (to come)	ven	Ven a mi casa (Come to my house)

Telling someone not do to something (tú/you) commands

You just learned how to tell someone to do something. Now you will learn how to tell someone *not to do something*!

To form a *"don't do that"* command, the following format is used:

hablar (-ar) + (es) = no *hables*

verb ending	Infinitive	tú command (don't do that)	Ejemplo
-ar	hablar (to talk)	no hables	No hables conmigo (Don't talk with me)

comer (-er) + (as) = no *comas*

verb ending	Infinitive	tú command (don't do that)	Ejemplo
-er	comer (to eat)	No comas	No comas dulces (Don't eat sweets)

escribir (-ir) (+ as) = no *escribas*

verb ending	Infinitive	tú command (don't do that)	Ejemplo
-ir	escribir (to write)	No escribas	No escribas la carta (Don't write the letter)

In summary (en resumen): As you can see, there is a very simple pattern when telling someone not to do something. You just put the opposite ending of the action word (+s). So you take "ar" and make it "es" and for "er" or "ir" it would be "as".

Recap

Telling someone **what to do** and **what not to do**

- **ar** (using *hablar*, to speak)

  • habla (tú)/ no hab**les** (tú) (speak/don't speak)

- **er** (using *comer*, to eat)**:**

  • come (tú)/ no co**mas** (tú) (eat/don't eat)

- **ir** (using *escribir*, to write)**:**

  • escribe (tú) / no escri**bas** (tú) (write/don't write)

Hay: means there is/are

Hay una casa grande en la esquina. = *There is* a big house in the corner.

Hay que + infinitive of action word "one must do something"

Hay que estudiar para tener éxito. = *One must* study to succeed.

Erin Ashley Sieber

¡CULTURA!

TIME ORIENTATION

Unlike in the North American culture, Latinos/Hispanics are not overly concerned with time. Being late **is not** considered rude or disrespectful. Instead it means that a person is giving priority to a more urgent situation. In the North American culture, wasting someone's time is considered rude, a major offense and some might even consider it an insult. In the Hispanic culture, tardiness is non-existent, since no one would be concerned with the time as such. The term "o'clock," or "en punto," is not referred to when establishing time frames. For example, 10:00 A.M. would mean to a Hispanic "around ten," not ten o'clock on the dot, thus arriving at ten after or quarter after ten would not be thought of as tardy in a Hispanic setting.

This culture difference really is true. To give you an example, when I first moved to Miami, Florida and made Latin(a) friends, we would make plans to go out and set a time to pick me up at. The first time I was ready to go at the time we decided on. Well 30 minutes went by and I was still waiting for them to pick me up, at which time I called to see if they were okay. When I called, they were still at home getting ready! I was floored! I couldn't understand how someone would think it is okay to arrive 45 minutes to an hour late. It happened a couple of times until I finally decided how to handle the situation. Whatever time they told me they would be at my house to pick me up is the time that **I would start getting ready** (NOT BE READY). This way I would avoid wasting time!

It is a cultural difference but as long as you are aware of it, you will avoid getting frustrated or upset about it!

Capítulo veinticuatro (Chapter 24) Flip it and Reverse it! ¡Da la vuelta y inviértalo!

What does a Spanish sentence look like?

If you heard:

"It I want" or "You I love"

You would understand, right? You might think that the person hadn't had proper English grammar lessons but the point is, you would understand ("It I want" = "I want it" and "You I love= "I love you"). If you understand, then you will not have a problem forming a Spanish sentence.

You probably might find this hard to believe but English sentence structure is actually more rigid than a Spanish sentence structure. This is good news for you, because you will be able to form a Spanish sentence in different ways:

> **The one principal thing to learn and remember**
> *is that in Spanish, the object of a sentence*
> *can come before the action word*

What does this mean? It means that a lot of the time, the sentence structure in Spanish is *reverse* to that of an English one.

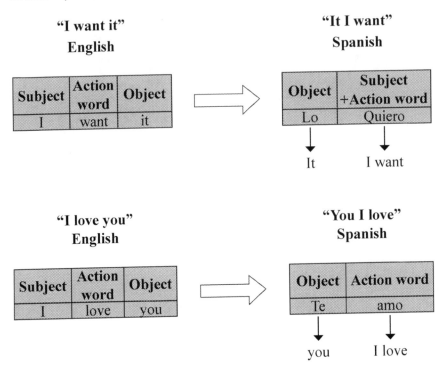

"I want it"
English

"It I want"
Spanish

Subject	Action word	Object
I	want	it

Object	Subject +Action word
Lo	Quiero

It   I want

"I love you"
English

"You I love"
Spanish

Subject	Action word	Object
I	love	you

Object	Action word
Te	amo

you   I love

However, not all Spanish sentences are reversed! You can speak Spanish the same way you speak English a lot of times and just translate your English sentence into Spanish. Let's look at how:

- I want → Quiero   to go → ir   to the movies → al cine

- I like → Me gusta   this → esta   song → canción

- I am → Estoy   in → en   a meeting → una reunión

168

The beauty about Spanish sentences is that the subject is contained in the action word, so instead of having to use an extra word like we do in English, it is all summed up in the action word!

Ejemplos:

Voy - I go
Hablamos - We speak
Viajan - They travel
Roncas - You snore

Mariachi is a form of folk music from Mexico. Mariachi began as a regional folk style called "Son Jaliscience" in the center west of Mexico originally played only with string instruments and musicians dressed in the white pants and shirts of peasant farmers. From the 19th to 20th century, migrations from rural areas into cities such as Guadalajara and Mexico City, along with the Mexican government's cultural promotion gradually re-labeled it as *Son* style, with its alternate name of "mariachi" becoming used for the "urban" form. Modifications of the music include influences from other music such as polkas and waltzes, the addition of trumpets and the use of charro outfits by mariachi musicians. The musical style began to take on national prominence in the first half of the 20th century, with its promotion at presidential inaugurations and on the radio in the 1920s. (http://en.wikipedia.org/wiki/Mariachi)

Spanish words that will confuse you at some point

agregar – to add
agarrar – to catch, to grab; to hold on to

Capítulo veinticinco (Chapter 25)

The Earth is Round! *And so is the way you can speak Spanish!*

The concept of a spherical Earth dates back to ancient Greek philosophy from around the 6th century BC, but remained a matter of philosophical speculation until the 3rd century BC when Hellenistic astronomy established the spherical shape of the earth as a physical given. A practical demonstration of Earth's spherical shape was achieved by Ferdinand Magellan and Juan Sebastian Elcano's expedition's circumnavigation (1519–1521). (http://en.wikipedia.org/wiki/Spherical_Earth)

So what does this mean? We move around the Earth in a round motion and you can also speak Spanish in a roundabout way! In other words, there are many ways to say the same thing in Spanish. **NOTE** This is a good thing! *Why you ask?* Because since you are not a native speaker and may not be able to learn every word in the Spanish language, or remember a certain word or phrase that you learned, you will still be able to communicate if you remember what The Gringa Way refers to as **"Talk in a Circle"**. This doesn't mean that you sit around speaking with people in a circle! What it is, is a way for you to be able to express yourself in a different or roundabout way with the use of more words than necessary to express an idea.

In the process of learning the language, you will do this a lot. There are times, where perhaps I can't think of a specific word(s) to express a concise thought, but I can come up with many other ways to express what I want to say.

Let's look at some ejemplos:

"I speak the language fluently" (Hablo la lengua con fluidez)

If you want to say this sentence but you forgot what the word for *fluently* is, you can talk around it in a circle and express this thought in a different way.

- Manejo la lengua perfectamente - I handle the language perfectly
- Manejo la lengua sin problemas - I handle the language without problems
- No tengo ningún problema hablando la lengua - I don't have any problem speaking the language

Ejemplo: "jewelry charm" (un encanto de joyas)

Let's say that you are talking with someone about a charm you bought for a new piece of jewelry. You really have to convey you bought a charm because there is really no other word for a charm. You can't think of the word and then you remember you can "talk in a circle"! You can describe it and talk around the word:

- adornos de los que se ponen en joyas - ornaments that are placed on jewelry
- una pequeña joya que adorna joyas para mujeres - a small jewel that adorns womens jewlery

Ejemplo: "The best Peruvian food" (La mejor comida peruana)

If you are in a conversation and are talking about where to get "the best Peruvian food" but you can't remember how to say "Peruvian" properly or any of the other words in the sentence, you can use these alternatives:

- La mejor comida viene de Peru - The best food comes from Peru

- La comida que se hacen los peruanos es la mejor - The food that Peruvians make is the best
- La comida hecha por Peruanos es riquísima - Food made by Peruvians is delicious

There are many examples but the most important thing is to remember you can always talk around a topic that you don't know a specific word(s) for but are trying to convey!

¡CULTURA!

The **Twelve Grapes** (The twelve grapes of luck) or as they are pronounced in Spanish, **Las doce uvas de la suerte**, is a Spanish tradition that dates back to at least 1895 but become consolidated in 1909. The tradition consists of eating a grape with each bell strike at midnight on December 31. This tradition was also adopted by places with a broad cultural relation with Spain, such as Mexico and other Latin American countries, as well as Hispanic communities in the United States. According to the tradition, this leads to a year of prosperity.

Capítulo veintiséis (Chapter 26)

Commonly Confused Words (palabras que se confunden frecuentamente)

This chapter has been left as the last one on purpose because if you would have been introduced to this material prior to now, you would have been even more confused than now. I wanted you to learn the nitty gritty first so you can take your knowledge and apply it to what you are about to learn.

Many people will walk around with a English/Spanish dictionary and look up a word when they don't how to say something. However, translating from English to Spanish using a dictionary can be challenging and fraught with the risk that you will make a serious mistake. Why? Because unlike *in English* where one word is the same for every context (**por ejemplo: to save**), *in Spanish there is seldomly more than one word that needs to be applied to the appropriate context of what you are saying.*

Therefore, (as mentioned in "Spanish is Literal but can not be translated literally" section) you should move forward learning the meaning of what you want to say, not word-for-word translation.

You have already learned this in the chapter with the action words,"ser and estar" (both meaning **to be**), "saber and conocer" (both meaning **"to know"**), and "pedir and preguntar" (both meaning **to ask**).

Here are some are words and action words that require a certain word depending on the context of what you are talking about.

To leave: salir y dejar

salir – "to leave" in the sense of **"exiting"** or **"going away"** **NOTE**
"an exit" in Spanish is called **una salida**, which comes from this action

word, salir) (Voy a salir de la casa de mi amiga más tarde - I am going to leave my friend's house later).

dejar – "to leave" in the sense of **"leaving an object somewhere"** (I left my books in the train. Dejé mis libros en el tren).

NOTE dejar also can mean "to leave" in the less common sense of **"to allow."** (Leave me go!¡Déjame salir!)

To take: llevar, tomar, sacar

llevar –"to take" in the sense of **"to carry"** or **"to transport."** (¿Vas a llevarme al aeropuerto? Are you going to take me to the airport?)

tomar – "to take" in the sense of **"to take for one's use"** (Tomo el coche al doctor. I take the car to the doctor).

sacar – "to take" in the sense of **"to take out something"** (El hombre sacó la basaura. The man took the trash out).

To play: jugar and tocar

jugar – "to play" in the sense of **"playing a game"** (Jugamos el fútbol cada semana. We play football every week).

tocar – "to play" in the sense of **"playing a musical instrument"** (I like playing the guitar. Me gusta tocar la guitarra.)

To apply: aplicar, aplicarse, solicitar

aplicar – to apply something (such as sunscreen, makeup, etc.) (Aplico el protector solar cuando voy a la playa. I apply sunscreen when I go to the beach.)

aplicarse – to apply oneself (in something) (Él mismo se aplicó a su tarea. He applied himself to his homework.)

solicitar – to apply for *(job, loan)*, (Solicité el préstamo de la casa hoy. I applied for the house loan today.) to request, to ask for (Solicité que mi novio pague la cuenta. I requested that my boyfriend pay the bill.)

To register, to sign up for something, to enroll

inscribirse – to enroll (for something)

registrarse – to register (to vote) (Me registré para votar. I registered to vote.)

apuntarse – to sign up, to join; put one's name down (Ella apuntó para una clase de yoga. She signed up for a yoga class)

matricularse – to enroll (oneself) in a college or university (Ella se matriculó en la clase española. She enrolled in the Spanish class.)

Spanish words that will confuse you at some point
el cojín – the cushion **el cajón** – the drawer

A Toast to Your Spanish Learning
Un brindis a su aprendizaje de español

Salud (Health)

Amor (Love)

Dinero (Money)

Y Tiempo Para Gozarlo

(And Time to Enjoy it All)

Recap of phrases and tips mentioned in book

-o ending Spanish words are masculine
-a ending Spanish words are feminine
el + numero + de + mes = the day of the month
es (singular) = It is
y = and
o = or
y cuarto = quarter pass an hour
a = at, to
al = at the, to the
de = of, from
del = of the, from the
el, la, los, las = the
un, una, unos, unas = a, an
es + el/la (+ word) = It is the _____
es + un/una (+ word) = It is a _____
son + los/las (+ word) = They are the _____
yo = I
tú = you (inf)
él, ella, usted = you (formal)
nosotros/as = we
ustedes = they, you all
lo = it
lo que = that which
este/esta = this
estos/estas = these
ese/esa = that
esos/esas = those
aquel/aquella = that over there
aquellos/aquellas = those over there
Gracias por = Thank you for
más = more
menos = less
ir + a + infinitive = to go to (action word)
tener que + infinitive form of verb = to have to (action word)
llevar (conjugated) + period of time = It has been (period of time)
hay = there is/there are
hay que + infinitive = one must (what must be done)

Most books include pages and pages of vocabulary in the back. This book is not one of them nor is it a Spanish/English dictionary. There have been many dictionaries published containing thousands and thousands of words. For a list of all Spanish words in the language, please refer to a dictionary. I am listing general vocabulary words for certain daily items, along with the key words that accompany them, in order to be able to form a thought or sentence.? I am doing this because usually when learning vocabulary, you are just taught the vocabulary words but not any other word that goes along with it in order to form a sentence.

Por ejemplo: if you learn the word for chair - *la silla*, what good will it be to you if you can't use it in a sentence? What is important is that you learn not only the word but that you can you this word to form a thought such as; "Sit in the chair." or "I like that chair." or "Move that chair please! This will be a lot more useful for you than just pointing and being able to say the word for the chair.

How do you say in Spanish_____ **¿Cómo se dice en español?**

Phrases for saying hi:

Hola

Welcome - Bienvenido (one person) Bienvendidos (more than one person)

Good morning - Buenos días

Good afternoon - Buenas tardes

Good evening - Buenas noches

What's new? - ¿Qué hay de nuevo?

How are you? - ¿Cómo estás?(informal) ¿Cómo está usted? (formal)

I'm fine, thanks. And you? - Bien gracias, ¿y tú? (informal) Bien gracias, ¿y usted? (formal)

I am very well, thank you - Estoy muy bien, gracias.

So so - así así

I am not very good - No estoy muy bien

<u>Way of introducing yourself/being introduced</u>

What is your name? ¿Cómo te llamas? (informal) ¿Cómo se llama usted? (formal)

My name is - Me llamo (name) or Mi nombre es (name).

Mr./Mrs./Miss - Señor/ Señora/ Señorita

Let me introduce you to (name of person) - Permítame presentarte a (name) (informal) Permítame presentarle a (name) (formal)

Nice to meet you - Encantado/a

              Mucho gusto

              ¡Tanto Gusto!

              Un placer conocerte (informal)

              Un placer conocerle (formal)

Where are you from? ¿De dónde eres? (informal) ¿De dónde es usted? (formal)

Where are you all from? ¿De dónde son ustedes?

I'm from (name of place you are from) - Soy de (place you are from)

I am (American) - Soy (americano/a)

How old are you? - ¿Cuántos años tienes? (informal)

¿Cuántos años tiene? (formal)

I'm (enter your age) years old - Tengo (enter age) años

Where do you live? - ¿Dónde vives? (inf)

¿Dónde vive? (form)

I live in (name of place where you live) - Vivo en (name of place where you live)

What do you do for a living? - ¿A qué te dedicas? (informal)

¿A qué se dedica? (formal)

I work as a (enter job) - Trabajo como (enter job)

Do you speak Spanish? ¿Hablas español? (informal)

¿Habla español? (formal)

Yes, I speak Spanish - Sí, hablo español

Practice Conversation

Greeting word/phrase: Hola (hi) ¿Qué tal? (How is it going?)

Greeting response: Buenos días (Good morning). Buenas tardes (Good afternoon). Buenas noches (Good evening)

Ask a persons name: ¿Cómo te llamas? (informal)

¿Cómo se llama? (formal)

Name response: Me llamo Enrique. (I am called Enrique.)

Pleased to meet you phrase: Mucho gusto (Pleasure to meet you).

Encantado(Enchanted to meet you)

Response: Igualmente (Likewise).

El gusto es mío (The pleasure is mine).

Ask how a person is: ¿Cómo estás **(tú)**? (How are you?) (informal)

¿Cómo está **usted**? (How are you?) (formal)

¿Qué tal? (What's up?) (informal)

Response: Bien (good)

Así así (so so)

Mal (bad)

Farewell: Adiós (good bye)

Hasta luego (Until later)

Hasta pronto (See you soon)

Hasta mañana (Until tomorrow)

<u>**Ways of saying goodbye**</u>

Goodbye - Adiós

See you later - Hasta luego

Hasta la vista

See you soon - Hasta pronto

See you tomorrow - Hasta mañana

See you next week - Hasta la proxima semana

Nos vemos la proxima semana

Have a nice day! –¡Que tengas un buen día! (inf)

¡Que tenga un buen día! (forml)

¡Que pases un buen día! (inf)

¡Que pase un buen día! (formal)

¡Que lo pases bien! (inf)

¡Que lo pase bien! (formal)

Good night - Buenas noches

I have to go - Tengo que irme

I will be right back - Regreso en un momentito

<u>**Ways of saying thank you**</u>

Thank you - Gracias

Much thanks - Muchas gracias

Very kind of you - Muy amable

You are welcome - De nada, no hay de que

Spanish Expressions and Words

Here you go! (when giving something)	¡Aquí tiene!
Do you like it?	¿Te gusta? ¿Te encanta?
I really like it!	¡Me gusta/ Me encanta!
Really!	¡Verdad!
Look!	¡Mira!
Hurry up!	¡Date prisa! ¡Apurate!
What? Where?	¿Qué? ¿Dónde?
What time is it?	¿Qué hora es?
Give me this!	¡Dame eso!
I love you!	¡Te quiero!
I feel sick.	Me siento mal.
I need a doctor	¡Necessito un médico!
Hey!	¡Oye!

Survival Spanish phrases

English	español (Spanish)
I don't understand	No entiendo No comprendo
Please speak more slowly	Por favor hable más despacio
Please write it down	¿Puede escribirlo, por favor?
Do you speak Spanish?	¿Habla usted español? (frm) ¿Hablas español? (inf)
Yes, a little	Sí, hablo un poquito Sí, un poquito
Excuse me	¡Perdón! ¡Perdone! ¡Discúlpe!
How much is this?	¿Cuánto cuesta? ¿Cuánto cuesta esto?

Sorry	¡Perdón! ¡Perdone! ¡Lo siento!
Where's the toilet?	¿Dónde está el baño? ¿Dónde están los sanitarios? ¿Dónde está el inodoro? ¿Dónde está el cuarto de baño?
Leave me alone!	¡Déjeme en paz!
Cheers!	¡Salud!

face and body/cara y cuerpo

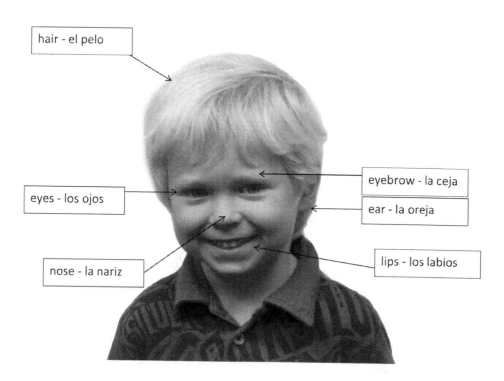

hair - el pelo

eyebrow - la ceja

ear - la oreja

eyes - los ojos

nose - la nariz

lips - los labios

clothes/la ropa

accessories - **los acessorios**
bathing suit - **traje de baño**
bathrobe - **la bata**
belt - **el cinturón**
blouse - **la blusa**
boots - **las botas**
coat - **el abrigo**
diaper - **la mantilla**
dress - **el vestido**
gloves - **los guantes**
Handkerchief - **el pañuelo**
hat- **el sombrero**
heels, high heels - **los tacones**
hosiery - **las medias**
jacket - **la chaqueta**
pajamas - **las pijamas**
pants - **los pantalones**
raincoat - **el impermeable**
sandals - **las sandalias**
scarf - **la bufanda**
shirt - **la camisa**
shoes - **los zapatos**
shorts - **los pantalones cortos**
skirt - **la falda**
socks - **los calcetines**
suit - **el traje**
sweat pants - **los pantalones sudadores**
sweatshirt - **la sudadera**
swim trunks - **el traje de baño**
tie - **la corbata**
tee shirt - **la camiseta**
underwear - **los calzones**
vest - **el chaleco**

family/la familia

- parents - **los padres**
- brother - **el hermano**
- sister - **la hermana**
- cousin - **el primo/la prima**
- uncle - **el tío**
- aunt - **la tía**
- great grandfather - **el bisabuelo**
- great grandmother - **la bisabuela**
- grandson - **el nieto**
- grandaughter - **la nieta**
- step-mother - **la madrastra**
- step-father - **el padrastro**
- stepbrother - **el hermanastro**
- stepsister - **la hermanastra**
- brother-in-law - **el cuñado**
- sister-in-law - **la cuñada**
- daughter-in-law - **la nuera**
- son-in-law - **el yerno**
- father-in-law - **el suegro**
- mother-in-law - **la suegra**
- half-brother - **medio hermano**
- half-sister - **media hermana**
- nephew - **el sobrino**

- niece - **la sobrina**
- relatives - **los parientes**
- the husband - **el esposo**
- the wife - **la esposa**

Other relationships

- friend - **el amigo/la amiga**
- best friend - **mejor amigo/a**
- pet - **la mascota**
- dog - **el perro**
- cat - **el gato**
- fish - **el pescado** (comida) **el pez** (animal)

house/la casa

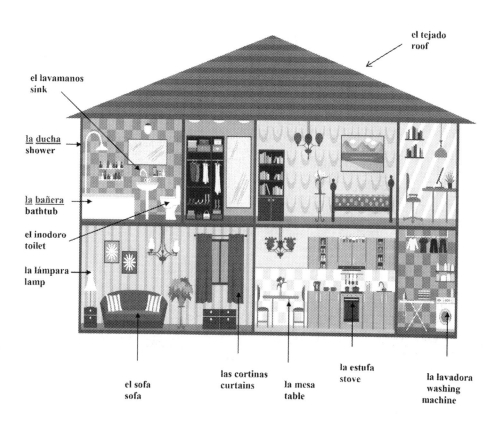

el tejado
roof

el lavamanos
sink

la ducha
shower

la bañera
bathtub

el inodoro
toilet

la lámpara
lamp

el sofa
sofa

las cortinas
curtains

la mesa
table

la estufa
stove

la lavadora
washing
machine

189

sports/los deportes

basketball- **el baloncesto**
baseball - el **béisbol**
football- **el fútbol americano**
swimming - **la natación**
bicycling - **el ciclismo**
bowling - **el juego de bolos**
golf - **el golf**
horeseback riding - **la equitación**
tennis - **el tenis**
boxing - **el boxeo**
skiing - **el esquiar**
snowboarding - **el snowboarding**
ice skating - **patinaje sobre hielo**
volleyball - **el volibol**
soccer - **el fútbol**

jugar - to play (a sport)
Ejemplo:
Juego el volibol - **I play** volleyball
Juegas el baloncesto - **You play** basketball
Ella **juega** el golf - **She plays** golf
Jugamos el beisbol - **We play** baseball
Ellos **juegan** el tenis - **They play** tennis

transportion/ el transporte

A pie: on foot
airplane: el avión
bicycle: la bicicleta
bus: el bus, el autobús
car: el coche
RV: la caravana (does that word look familiar to you?.....caravan!)
helicopter: el helicóptero
motorcycle: la motocicleta (you can also just say **la moto**)
subway: el metro
taxi: el taxi
train: el tren

To say you are going by a certain means of transportation:

Voy en_____ (mode of transportation)
Vas en_____
Va en_____
Vamos en_____
Van en_____

To say you are going to take:

Voy a tomar ___(mode of transportation):
Vas a tomar _____
Va a tomar_____
Vamos a tomar_____
Van a tomar_____

What do you call people from a given country? Most of us US-Americans probably don't even know what to call somebody from a different state! What do you call a person from Tennessee?... from Maryland???... from Rhode Island?

	A *man* from the given country.	A *female* from the given country.	2 or more *males* or a mixed *group of men* & *women* from the given country.	Two or more *women* from the given country
Argentina	argentino	argentina	argentinos	argentinas
Belice	Beliciano	beliciana	belicianos	belicianas
Bolivia	boliviano	boliviana	bolivianos	bolivianas
Chile	chileno	chilena	chilenos	chilenas
Colombia	colombiano	colombiana	colombianos	colombianas
Costa Rica	costarricense	costarricense	costarricenses	costarricenses
	costarriqueño	costarriqueña	costarriqueños	costarriqueñas
Cuba	cubano	cubana	cubanos	cubanas
Ecuador	ecuatoriano	ecuatoriana	ecuatorianos	ecuatorianas
Ecuatorial Guinea	Guineano	guineana	guineanos	guineanas
El Salvador	salvadoreño	salvadoreña	salvadoreños	salvadoreñas
España	español	española	espanoles	españolas
Guatemala	guatematelco	guatematelca	guatematelcos	guatematelcas
Honduras	hondureño	hondureña	hondureños	hondureñas
México	mexicano	mexicana	mexicanos	mexicanas

Nicaragua	nicaragüense	nicaragüense	nicaragüenses	nicaragüenses
	nicaragüeño	nicaragüeña	nicaragüeños	nicaragüeñas
Panamá	panameño	panameña	panameños	panameñas
Paraguay	paraguayo	paraguaya	paraguayos	paraguayas
	paraguayano	paraguayana	paraguayanos	paraguayanas
Perú	peruano	peruana	peruanos	peruanas
Puerto Rico	puertorriqueño	puertorriqueña	puertorriqueños	puertorriqueñas
Republica Dominicana	dominicano	dominicana	dominicanos	dominicanas
Uruguay	uruguayo	uruguaya	uruguayos	uruguayas
Venezuela	venezolano	venezolana	venezolanos	venezolanas

Helpful Tips Remember that to say **I am Argentian, I am Mexican, etc.** = **Yo soy aregentina, Yo soy mexicano, etc.**

Tip: Remember that to ask someone where they are from you say:

De donde eres? (informal)

De donde es? (formal)

To say I am from (country) = Yo soy de (Argentina). Yo soy de (Mexico). etc.

Photography credits

Special thank you to Saara Gaboury for the creation of "The Gringa" logo and artwork

Stock Photos:

mirror image
Image ID: 80436856
Copyright: weissdesign
Purchase with Receipt

Holstein cow, 5 years old, standing in front of white background
Image ID: 84468490
Copyright: Eric Isselee
Purchase with Receipt

female english bulldog puppy wrapped up in pink with reflection on white background
Image ID: 62356723
Copyright: WilleeCole Photography
Purchase with Receipt

english bulldog puppy wearing plaid shirt and trucker hat with reflection on white background
Image ID: 63120031
Copyright: WilleeCole Photography
Purchase with Receipt

Happy Cinco De Mayo. Happy pepper singing
Image ID: 28828076
Copyright: Laurie Barr
Purchase with Receipt

A business woman talks with a business man in office with a bookshelf and white wall as background

Image ID: 78499108
Copyright: Shirley Ren
Purchase with Receipt

Helpful tips and advice on a yellow office note with a red thumb tack representing the concept of good client business service.
Image ID: 74943355
Copyright: Lightspring
Purchase with Receipt

Quinceañera Tiara
Image ID: 37691419
Copyright: Gema Duran
Purchase with Receipt

time out take a break leasure time off relaxation taking a holliday
Image ID: 166877111
Copyright: Dirk Ercken
Purchase with Receipt

3D render of grandparents with grandchildren
Image ID: 142339033
Copyright: Gouraud Studio
Purchase with Receipt

Remember - Stock Image
Stock Photo: 1672717
Mariachi Band - Stock Image
Vetta Stock Photo: 19526976
Daisies on a Spring Green Background - Stock Image
Stock Photo: 18940690
Fall Leaves With Pumpkin - Stock Image
Stock Photo: 909714
Male symbol - Stock Image

Stock Photo: 13157781
Female Symbol. - Stock Image
Stock Photo: 11441735
Birth Of Idea - Stock Image
Stock Photo: 19886792
Beach with smiling sun - Stock Image
Stock Photo: 16466102
lucky grapes tradition - Illustration
Stock Illustration: 14566732
house in a cut - Illustration
Stock Illustration: 20018930
Wine Glasses - Stock Image
Stock Photo: 24316302

Works Cited

http://www.careerbuilder.com/Article/CB-163-Getting-Ahead-Bilingual-Youre-Valuable
Source: **United States Census 2010**
http://en.wikipedia.org/wiki/Gringo

(http://en.wikipedia.org/wiki/Cuban_espresso)

(Source: http://en.wikipedia.org/wiki/Phonetics)
(http://en.m.wikipedia.org/wiki/Don_Quixote_1605.gif)
(http://en.wikipedia.org/wiki/Mattel)
(http://en.wikipedia.org/wiki/Uno_(card_game)

(http://en.wikipedia.org/wiki/Plaza_Mayor,_Madrid)
(http://en.wikipedia.org/wiki/Taco_Bell)
(http://en.wikipedia.org/wiki/All_Night_Long_(All_Night)
(http://en.wikipedia.org/wiki/Three_Amigos)
(Source: http://en.wikipedia.org/wiki/Livin'_la_Vida_Loca)
(http://en.wikipedia.org/wiki/Taco_bell)
(http://en.wikipedia.org/wiki/The_Who)

(http://en.wikipedia.org/wiki/LittleHavana)

(http://en.wikipedia.org/wiki/Nuthin'_but_a_'G'_Thang)

(http://en.wikipedia.org/wiki/West_Side_Story)

(http://en.wikipedia.org/wiki/Mariachi)

(http://en.wikipedia.org/wiki/Spherical_Earth)